Learning Search-driven Application Development with SharePoint 2013

Build optimum search-driven applications using SharePoint 2013's new and improved search engine

Johnny Tordgeman

PUBLISHING

BIRMINGHAM - MUMBAI

Learning Search-driven Application Development with SharePoint 2013

First published: July 2013

Production Reference: 2050713

Published by Packt Publishing Ltd.
Livery Place
35 Livery Street
Birmingham B3 2PB, UK.

ISBN 978-1-78217-100-3

www.packtpub.com

Cover Image by David Gimenez (bilbaorocker@yahoo.co.uk)

Credits

Author

Johnny Tordgeman

Reviewer

Samuel Zuercher [MVP]

Acquisition Editor

Aarthi Kumaraswamy

Commissioning Editor

Meeta Rajani

Technical Editors

Anita Nayak

Sonali S. Vernekar

Copy Editors

Insiya Morbiwala

Aditya Nair

Alfida Paiva

Laxmi Subramanian

Project Coordinator

Amey Sawant

Proofreader

Marla Gould

Indexer

Rekha Nair

Graphics

Abhinash Sahu

Production Coordinator

Nitesh Thakur

Cover Work

Nitesh Thakur

About the Author

Johnny Tordgeman is the CTO of E4D Solutions Ltd., a boutique development and consulting firm in Israel. Johnny specializes in architecting enterprise-level solutions built on top of Microsoft's SharePoint platform. Johnny utilizes the latest in web technology and methodology in his solutions, such as HTML5, SPA, and MVC4.

Johnny is the author of *MCTS: Microsoft Silverlight 4 Development (70-506) Certification Guide, Packt Publishing*, which was published in 2012.

Johnny is a skilled lecturer and a Microsoft-certified trainer and can be found speaking at various conferences, open houses, and user groups.

You can always find Johnny at `http://blog.johnnyt.me`, on Twitter at `@JTordgeman`, and on LinkedIn at `http://www.linkedin.com/in/johnnytor`.

I would like to dedicate this book to my son Roy and wife Ayelet. You two are my source of inspiration and the best family I could have ever hoped for.

First and foremost, I would like to thank Meeta Rajani and Sneha Modi, my amazing editors. Without your help and support, this book wouldn't have happened!

My dear family – Itzik, Varda, Yuval, and Shirly, and friends – Idan, Yossi, Rani, Leon, Niv, Guy, Tal, Eyal, Itay, and Tung (Tony) Pham. Thank you for the moral support and late nights we spent together. This book and I owe a great deal to all of you.

About the Reviewer

Samuel Zuercher [MVP] (SharePoint MVP since 2011) works as a Senior Consultant at Experts Inside, Switzerland, an international company he founded with another SharePoint MVP, Christian Glessner. He has been working with SharePoint since early 2006 and has in-depth knowledge from Version 2.0 onward. He also holds certifications for every SharePoint version since then. As a Microsoft Certified Trainer, he often trains people, from end users to technical specialists. Additionally, he founded the Swiss SharePoint Community, is one of the main drivers of Collaboration Days, and runs the blog sharepointszu.com. He speaks about SharePoint in a variety of events all over the world. In his job, he is involved in many SharePoint projects from concept to rollout and has a lot of experience. His specialty is information and system architecture, no-code solutions, and social collaboration. You can reach him via e-mail at szu@expertsinside.com, Twitter at @SharePointSzu, or a variety of platforms such as Xing, LinkedIn, or Facebook.

www.PacktPub.com

Support files, eBooks, discount offers and more

You might want to visit www.PacktPub.com for support files and downloads related to your book.

Did you know that Packt offers eBook versions of every book published, with PDF and ePub files available? You can upgrade to the eBook version at www.PacktPub.com and as a print book customer, you are entitled to a discount on the eBook copy. Get in touch with us at service@packtpub.com for more details.

At www.PacktPub.com, you can also read a collection of free technical articles, sign up for a range of free newsletters and receive exclusive discounts and offers on Packt books and eBooks.

http://PacktLib.PacktPub.com

Do you need instant solutions to your IT questions? PacktLib is Packt's online digital book library. Here, you can access, read and search across Packt's entire library of books.

Why Subscribe?

- Fully searchable across every book published by Packt
- Copy and paste, print and bookmark content
- On demand and accessible via web browser

Free Access for Packt account holders

If you have an account with Packt at www.PacktPub.com, you can use this to access PacktLib today and view nine entirely free books. Simply use your login credentials for immediate access.

Instant Updates on New Packt Books

Get notified! Find out when new books are published by following @PacktEnterprise on Twitter, or the *Packt Enterprise* Facebook page.

Table of Contents

Preface

Learning Search-driven Application Development with SharePoint 2013 is a fast-paced, practical, hands-on guide to the world of enterprise search in SharePoint 2013. With step-by-step tutorials and real-world-based exercises, this book will give you a head start in creating fresh and exciting search-driven applications using SharePoint 2013's new search engine. The book covers a wide range of topics such as Query Rules, Result Types and Display Templates, Working with the new client APIs, and Business Connectivity Services.

What this book covers

Chapter 1, Getting Started With SharePoint 2013 Search, gives you a taste of the new features SharePoint 2013 search brings to the table and then dives deep into the architecture that holds this system together.

Chapter 2, Using the Out of the Box Search Components, shows you how to use query rules and result sources and get a taste of building a simple search-driven application. SharePoint 2013 provides a rich out of the box experience for developing search-driven applications.

Chapter 3, Using the New CSOM and RESTful APIs, explains how to work with these new APIs and build a SharePoint hosted search-driven app using the new App developing approach. SharePoint 2013 changes the way we developers extend the platform by providing a whole new set of client-based APIs.

Chapter 4, Customizing the Look, focuses on creating display templates that define how a search result will render, and result types that define which display template a result should have. SharePoint 2013 opens up a whole new way to design our search results.

Chapter 5, *Extending Beyond SharePoint*, introduces how to create an external indexing connector and understand how to work with external data. In a real-world environment, not all the information we wish to search for is hosted within SharePoint. Business Connectivity Services (or BCS for short) enables us to extend beyond the realms of SharePoint and index data from external systems.

What you need for this book

To run the examples shown in this book you will need a SharePoint 2013 server with Visual Studio 2012 installed.

If you don't have access to a full SharePoint 2013 server, Office 365's SharePoint Online and Visual Studio 2012 can also be used to run most of the examples in this book.

Who this book is for

This book is written for SharePoint and JavaScript developers who wish to get started working with SharePoint search. The book assumes working knowledge with previous versions of SharePoint and some experience with JavaScript and client-side development.

Conventions

In this book, you will find a number of styles of text that distinguish between different kinds of information. Here are some examples of these styles, and an explanation of their meaning.

Code words in text, database table names, folder names, filenames, file extensions, pathnames, dummy URLs, user input, and Twitter handles are shown as follows: "We can include other contexts through the use of the `include` directive."

A block of code is set as follows:

```
[default]
exten => s,1,Dial(Zap/1|30)
exten => s,2,Voicemail(u100)
exten => s,102,Voicemail(b100)
exten => i,1,Voicemail(s0)
```

When we wish to draw your attention to a particular part of a code block, the relevant lines or items are set in bold:

```
[default]
exten => s,1,Dial(Zap/1|30)
exten => s,2,Voicemail(u100)
exten => s,102,Voicemail(b100)
exten => i,1,Voicemail(s0)
```

Any command-line input or output is written as follows:

```
# cp /usr/src/asterisk-addons/configs/cdr_mysql.conf.sample
    /etc/asterisk/cdr_mysql.conf
```

New terms and **important words** are shown in bold. Words that you see on the screen, in menus or dialog boxes for example, appear in the text like this: "clicking the **Next** button moves you to the next screen".

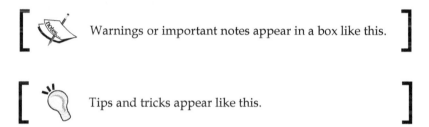

Warnings or important notes appear in a box like this.

Tips and tricks appear like this.

Reader feedback

Feedback from our readers is always welcome. Let us know what you think about this book—what you liked or may have disliked. Reader feedback is important for us to develop titles that you really get the most out of.

To send us general feedback, simply send an e-mail to feedback@packtpub.com, and mention the book title via the subject of your message.

If there is a topic that you have expertise in and you are interested in either writing or contributing to a book, see our author guide on www.packtpub.com/authors.

Customer support

Now that you are the proud owner of a Packt book, we have a number of things to help you to get the most from your purchase.

Downloading the example code

You can download the example code files for all Packt books you have purchased from your account at http://www.packtpub.com. If you purchased this book elsewhere, you can visit http://www.packtpub.com/support and register to have the files e-mailed directly to you.

Errata

Although we have taken every care to ensure the accuracy of our content, mistakes do happen. If you find a mistake in one of our books—maybe a mistake in the text or the code—we would be grateful if you would report this to us. By doing so, you can save other readers from frustration and help us improve subsequent versions of this book. If you find any errata, please report them by visiting http://www.packtpub.com/submit-errata, selecting your book, clicking on the **erratasubmissionform** link, and entering the details of your errata. Once your errata are verified, your submission will be accepted and the errata will be uploaded on our website, or added to any list of existing errata, under the Errata section of that title. Any existing errata can be viewed by selecting your title from http://www.packtpub.com/support.

Piracy

Piracy of copyright material on the Internet is an ongoing problem across all media. At Packt, we take the protection of our copyright and licenses very seriously. If you come across any illegal copies of our works, in any form, on the Internet, please provide us with the location address or website name immediately so that we can pursue a remedy.

Please contact us at copyright@packtpub.com with a link to the suspected pirated material.

We appreciate your help in protecting our authors, and our ability to bring you valuable content.

Questions

You can contact us at questions@packtpub.com if you are having a problem with any aspect of the book, and we will do our best to address it.

1
Getting Started with SharePoint 2013 Search

SharePoint 2013 feels like a breeze of fresh air, offering many new features and changes over older versions. In addition to a whole new social experience, a new development model called Apps, and native HTML5 support, SharePoint 2013 introduces a new and improved search engine. As the title of the book implies, this book is all about the new search engine. In this introductory chapter we will get a taste of the new features SharePoint 2013 Search brings to the table and then deep-dive into the architecture that holds this system together.

In this chapter, we will cover the following topics:

* New features of SharePoint 2013 Search
* The new search architecture

New features of SharePoint 2013 Search

The SharePoint 2013 Search engine is the most powerful enterprise search engine Microsoft has created to date. With this new release, Microsoft combined all of the best features of the legacy SharePoint Enterprise search engine with the best features of the FAST search engine, which Microsoft acquired back in 2008.

The new features of SharePoint 2013 Search can be divided into four main categories as follows:

* Search administration
* UI changes and customization
* Relevance and ranking features
* New development methods

Search administration

One drawback of search in previous versions of SharePoint was that almost everything had to be managed from the central administration page, which meant that search was managed at the farm level.

SharePoint 2013 changed that by adding most of the search settings from the farm level to site collections and sites (SPWebs). As SharePoint 2013 is offered as a cloud service (through Office 365), and cloud users have no access to settings in the farm-administration level, this was a welcome change that both cloud and on-premise site administrations can take advantage of.

Let's have a look at what settings are available for us to administrate; these are shown in the following screenshot:

Search
Result Sources
Result Types
Query Rules
Schema
Search Settings
Searchable columns
Search and offline availability
Configuration Import
Configuration Export

We will discuss these settings in detail in *Chapter 2, Using the Out of the Box Search Components*, but for now just keep in mind that a site administrator can configure the search experience on his/her site in ways that were reserved exclusively to farm administrators in previous versions.

In addition, Microsoft introduces a new crawling mode, continuous crawl. Continuous crawl helps to keep the search index as fresh as possible by crawling SharePoint sites (and only SharePoint sites) every 15 minutes, by default; we can change this value using PowerShell, as shown in the following snippet:

```
$ssa = Get-SPEnterpriseSearchServiceApplication
$ssa.SetProperty("ContinuousCrawlInterval",<minutes>)
```

The value we use for <minutes> is the number of minutes between crawling.

When running, the crawler gets changes from the crawled SharePoint sites and pushes them to the content processing component, which will process the new content on the fly.

By enabling the continuous crawler, items appear in the search almost immediately after being crawled.

UI changes and customization

If there is one change in SharePoint 2013 Search that just pops to the eyes, it is the new and fresh user interface (UI). If you worked with SharePoint 2010 search, you'll remember the following screenshot, showing a search-results page:

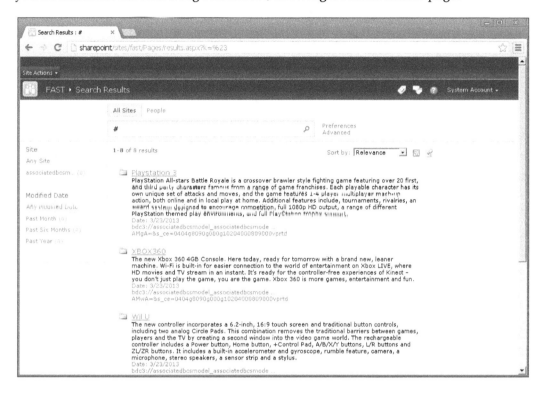

By looking at the preceding screenshot, we can see that it sports a pretty simple UI. We have textual refinements on the left side; predefined search scopes for websites and people (**All Sites** and **People**) on top, and a main, simply styled results area without grouping or categorization of results.

To customize the way the results are shown, we had to use XSL/XSLT, which is quite a messy and unattractive way to design.

Fast forward to the present day. The following screenshot displays how the results page looks like in SharePoint 2013:

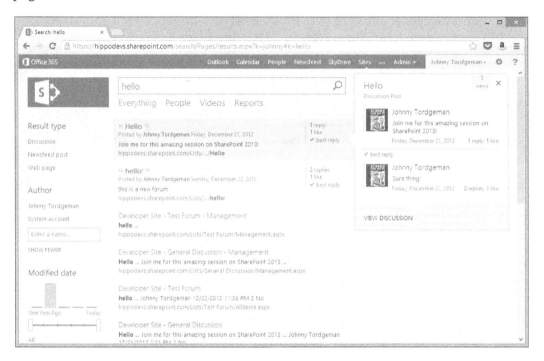

Now that's quite different, isn't it? The UI is modern thanks to the use of HTML and JavaScript templates. Instead of messing around with XSLT, we now have display templates to design our results using languages we already know and love: HTML, JavaScript, and CSS.

Take a look at the refinement panel on the left. While we still have textual refiners, we also have graphical ones, such as a scroller for dates.

We have new out-of-the-box search scopes — **Videos** and **Reports** — and results are grouped by their types; for example, the first two results are discussion items from a discussion board.

The biggest and most notable change, however, is the new hover panel. Whenever we hover over a search result, we are presented with a floating panel containing additional information about the hovered item. As SharePoint 2013 seamlessly integrates with Office web apps, any Office document we hover over will show a preview of its content in the new hover panel. The most important thing about the hover panel, however, is that we, as developers, have complete control over the content of this hover panel. Just like search results, the hover panel is also controlled by HTML, CSS, and JavaScript.

We will discuss all of these new and exciting customizations features in detail in *Chapter 4*, *Customizing the Look*.

Relevance and ranking features

As mentioned earlier, SharePoint 2013 Search took the best features of SharePoint Search and FAST and improved them. As such, SharePoint 2013 uses new and improved ranking models to determine which items are to be displayed and what would be their rank (the order in which they are displayed).

The key to successfully determine the relevancy of search results is to satisfy the intent of the person who issues the query. Let's explain this statement with an example; say I'm performing a search for Apple. Now, did I search for apple the fruit or Apple the technology company?

SharePoint 2013 Search continuously tracks and analyzes search usage to determine how content is connected, how often an item appears in search results, and which search results people click in order to continuously improve the relevance of items to the search query. So, if I clicked on a lot of fruit-related results, the search engine will assume I was looking for apple the fruit, and not the technology company.

We will discuss these new features in *Chapter 2*, *Using the Out of the Box Search Components*, and *Chapter 3*, *Using the New CSOM and RESTful APIs*.

New development methods

With this new release of SharePoint, Microsoft made changes to the search-development model. The old SOAP web service (ASMX) has been deprecated alongside the SQL query syntax that we could use to query against SharePoint data.

But, just like the the old saying goes, "out with the old and in with the new", we get some new features to play with to replace the ones that are gone.

- A new **Client Side Object Model (CSOM)** object which enable us to access the search service using JavaScript and C#. With the help of the search CSOM, we can create search-driven applications even for servers that don't have SharePoint 2013 installed on them.

- A dedicated **Representational State Transfer (REST)** service that enables us to execute queries against the search service from client applications using libraries such as jQuery or RestSharp. The REST service supports all of the properties available in the CSOM object, but instead of working against objects, we use the URL's query string to send parameters to it.

- An enhanced keyword query language with new and improved operators such as ONEAR and XRANK.

- Enhancements to the Business Connectivity Services Connector Framework, which improves capturing and logging of exceptions to help us troubleshoot errors during the crawl process.

We will discuss all of these topics in detail in *Chapter 3, Using the New CSOM and RESTful APIs*, and *Chapter 5, Extending Beyond SharePoint*.

Now that we have a general idea about what's new in SharePoint 2013 Search, let's go ahead and discuss the architecture that makes all of this happen.

The search architecture

SharePoint 2013 Search introduces a new search architecture that includes significant changes and new additions compared to previous versions. Since Microsoft consolidated FAST and SharePoint Search, the new search architecture has inherited components from both products while maintaining high scalability and performance.

Let's have a look at the new search architecture and discuss its components; refer to the following screenshot:

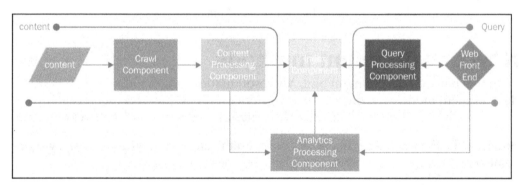

As we can see from the diagram, the search architecture can be divided into four components groups as follows:

- Content components
- Query components
- The index component
- The analytics-processing component

Content components

The content components are in charge of getting content ready for indexing. Each component has a well-defined role, which we will discuss next.

Crawl component

The crawl component is responsible for crawling content sources. It is the first stop for data that is about to be indexed by the search engine. The crawl component invokes connectors (both out-of-the-box and custom ones) that interact with the content source in order to crawl it.

While indexing, the crawl component uses one (or more) crawl database to temporarily store detailed tracking and historical information about the crawled item, such as the last time the item was crawled and the type of update during the last crawl.

Once an item is crawled, meaning both its data and its associated metadata is crawled, the crawl component delivers it to the content-processing component.

Content-processing component

The content-processing component's job is to analyze content it receives from the crawl component and feed it to the index component for indexing.

Content analysis is done by following a flow known as the Content Processing Flow, which is depicted in the following diagram:

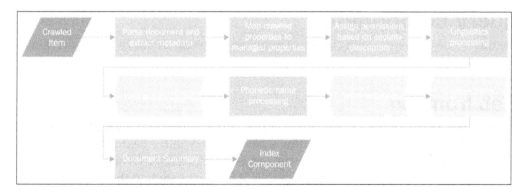

The rectangular blocks in the diagram represent stages that we cannot interact with. We won't be discussing them as they are quite self-explanatory. The curved rectangular blocks, however, represent stages that we can interact with during the processing flow.

The **Web service callout** stage is similar to the pipeline extensibility stage of FAST for SharePoint 2010, and allows you to add a callout from the content-processing component to a web service of your own so you can manipulate the crawled content before it gets indexed by the index component.

Unlike FAST's pipeline-extensibility stage, where code had to be executed in a sandbox, the web service callout accepts a web service endpoint, which is much easier and reduces the overhead involved in writing a console application to accompany the content-flow process.

Calling a web service during the processing stage can be useful for two scenarios.

- Creating new refiners by extracting data from unstructured text using our own logic
- Calculating new refiners based on the data of managed properties

You can find a great example on using the web service callout in Kathrine Hammervold's post, *Customize the SharePoint 2013 search experience with a Content Enrichment web service*, located at `http://blogs.msdn.com/b/sharepointdev/archive/2012/11/13/customize-the-sharepoint-2013-search-experience-with-a-content-enrichment-web-service.aspx`.

The next point of interaction is the word-breaking stage, which allows you to write your own custom word-breaking logic for the content processor. Please refer to the MSDN documentation on custom word breakers, located at `http://msdn.microsoft.com/en-us/library/jj163981.aspx`.

Query components

The query components are in charge of analyzing the search query and processing the results.

Web frontend

The web frontend is where the search process actually begins. A user can interact with the search service by either writing a search query in the search center (or a search box) or developing against the new public APIs: REST/OData services and the CSOM. Both the search center and public APIs are hosted on the frontend.

Once the user creates a query, the query is sent to the query-processing component for analysis. The query-processing component analyzes the query and forwards it to the index component. The index component returns the matching results to the query-processing component for another analysis and from there the results are forwarded to the web frontend to be displayed.

Query processing component

As mentioned previously, the query-processing component's job is to analyze and process both search queries and results.

When the query-processing component receives a search query from the frontend, it analyzes it in an attempt to optimize its precision and relevance. A site administrator can interact with a query using different techniques such as query rules or result source. We will discuss these techniques in detail in the next chapter, but for now it is important to understand that these manipulations are handled within the query-processing components. As part of its query handling, the query-processing component performs linguistic processes on the query, such as word-breaking and stemming.

Once the query is optimized, it is sent to the index component, which will process the optimized query and return a result set back to the query-processing component and from there to the search frontend.

The index component

The index component is the heart of the search service, and without proper planning it can easily become the bottleneck of the service as well.

The index component has the following two roles:

- **Input**: The index component is in charge of writing the optimized content it gets from the content-processing component to the index file
- **Output**: The index component is in charge of returning results from the index file to the query-processing component, by request

How the index component saves and manages this index file is out of the scope of this book, but you can read more about this in the TechNet article *Manage the index component in SharePoint Server 2013*, located at `http://technet.microsoft.com/en-us/library/jj862355.aspx`.

Analytics processing component

The analytics-processing component is a new addition to SharePoint Search. Its role is to analyze both content and user actions with the content in order to improve the search relevance for the user.

The analytics architecture consists of three main parts, as follows:

- The analytics-processing component, which runs the analytics jobs.
- The analytics-reporting database, which stores statistical information such as usage data.
- The link database, which stores information about searches and crawled documents. In addition, the link database is shared with the Content Processing Component, which in turn stores links and anchors in it. The information, the content-processing component stores is later used by the analytics-processing component.

The analytics-processing component runs two types of analytics: search analytics and usage analytics. The search analytics analyzes content from the content-processing component for information such as links, information related to people, and recommendations. The usage analytics analyzes user actions on an item, such as the number of views it had or how many users clicked on it.

An important output of usage analytics are the recommendations. The recommendations analysis creates recommendations on items based on how users have interacted with this specific item in the past. The analysis calculates an item-to-item relationship graph and updates it continuously based on search usage.

Keep in mind that the analytics-processing component is a "learning" component, which means it learns by usage. The more usage the search system will have, the better analytics it will provide.

Summary

This chapter marks the beginning of our journey to create search-driven applications using SharePoint 2013. We started the chapter by discussing the new features of SharePoint 2013 Search and divided them into four categories: administration changes, UI changes, relevance and ranking changes, and new development methods. Once we had an idea about what's new in SharePoint 2013 Search, we went on and deep-dived into the new search architecture.

In the next chapter we will get our hands dirty, and once we understand how to work with the out-of-the-box search components, we will build our first search-driven application using them.

2
Using the Out of the Box Search Components

Now that we know what's under the hood, let's get started with what we can do with it! In the previous chapter, we briefly mentioned the new search settings for sites and site collections. This chapter will dive deep into these settings. We will discuss the administrative side of SharePoint Search where we can define query rules and result sources and demonstrate the use of out of the box search components in a search-driven application.

In this chapter we will cover the following topics:

- Getting acquainted with result sources
- Learning query rules
- Using the content search web part
- Building a simple search-driven app

Getting acquainted with result sources

The best way to explain what a result source is, is by using a real life example.

Say you need to buy some milk. You know that you need to go to the supermarket and look for milk in the dairy department. You aren't going to be looking for milk in the tools department or even other areas of the store (such as the fruits and vegetables departments); you limit yourself to just the dairy department.

A result source acts the same. It allows you to restrict search queries to a specific subset of content from the search index by defining a set of rules that must be met by the content in order to show up as a result.

If the result source sounds familiar to you, it is because you have already encountered it before. Take a look at the following screenshot taken from the default SharePoint 2013 search center:

Below the search box we have four search verticals. These verticals are actually using result sources. Think about the **Videos** vertical. It takes your search query and looks for files in the **Local SharePoint Sites** content source and ends up with a known video file extension, that is, MP4.

A result source can be created at either the site, the site collection, or the application service (farm) level. This allows even site owners to create and manage customized search experiences for their users.

When creating a result source, we must specify which protocol (search provider) we wish to use. The four available protocols are as follows:

- **Local SharePoint**: The search index of the local SharePoint farm.
- **Remote SharePoint**: The search index of the remote SharePoint farm.
- **OpenSearch 1.0/1.1**: An external search provider that implements the OpenSearch protocol. An example of such a provider is Bing.com.
- **Exchange**: An Exchange Web Services endpoint.

In addition to protocol, we can specify a query text; this is basically a query that will run against the selected protocol to narrow down the results. For example, the following query will return all the PDF files that contain the following search term:

```
{searchTerms} fileextension:pdf
```

A result source, in many cases, is the heart of a search-driven application as it guarantees that only results that meet the specified rule be returned upon query.

Learning query rules

Query rules are a hot new feature of SharePoint 2013 search. In essence, query rules are the infrastructure for query pipeline extensibility. Using query rules, we can create conditional rules that will intelligently respond to what the user is trying to search for.

Let's assume we have a knowledge center site that tags all of its assets (videos, images, documents, and so on) using the following taxonomy dictionary as shown in the following screenshot:

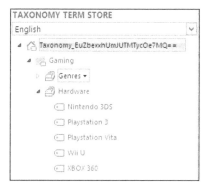

If a user searches for one of these terms, we should display a result on top of the other results, pointing the user to the knowledge center. A result that will always appear on top of other results is called a promoted result.

Promoted results are very similar to SharePoint 2010's best bets, but with one key difference: promoted results can react to taxonomy terms as well as matched keywords.

A promoted result, for the knowledge center we mentioned previously, will look as shown in the following screenshot:

Now, let's assume the user has searched for xbox 360 pictures. If a user has combined the terms "xbox 360" and "pictures" in a query, he/she is probably looking for pictures of the Xbox 360 console and not a document titled xbox 360 pictures. Using query rules, we can recognize the user's intent and act accordingly.

Since the user wanted pictures of the product, we added a nice block of results to the page, showing pictures of the product. This scenario will look as shown in the following screenshot:

Result blocks don't have to appear on top of all search results, like promoted results. We can also add ranked result blocks. Ranked result blocks are result blocks that appear among regular ranked results. Their rank among other results is based upon usage. The more the items inside a ranked block get clicked, the higher the block will be shown in the results page.

Creating query rules

Query rules can be defined at either the site, the site collection, or the service application (farm) level. To create a query rule, just head up to either the site or site collection's **Site Settings** page (or the search service application) and click on **Query Rules** under the **Search** Section.

When creating a query rule, you have to ask yourself the following three questions:

1. What search vertical (result source) is the user going to use?
2. Under which conditions should the query rule fire?
3. When the condition fires, what should the query rule do?

Now that we know how to plan our query rule, it's time to discuss how to put the planning into practice.

Setting the result source

First, we have to set the result source we are going to use for the query rule. This is done in the **Manage Query Rules** page shown in the following screenshot:

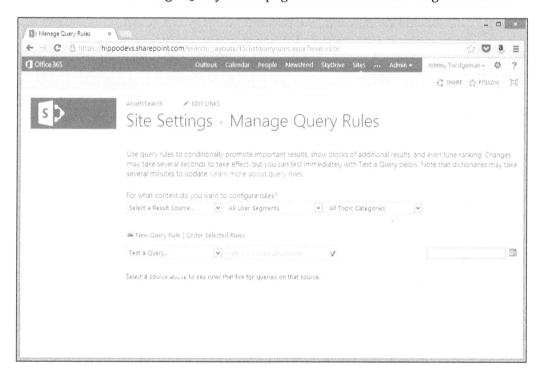

The upper row of dropdowns is used to set the context of the query. The context consists of a result source (first question), a user segment, and categories. In most cases, you'll only have to set the result source.

You may now ask yourself: what if I want to target the "Everything" search vertical and not a specific result source so that no matter what my users will search for, I can react to it?. Well, the answer is simple: use the **Local SharePoint Results (System)** result source.

The **Local SharePoint Results** result source is one of 16 out of the box result sources that ships with SharePoint 2013 and is the default search vertical of any search center. Among the other out of the box result sources, you'll find **Documents** that narrows the search scope to document files only, **Local People Search** for people-related results, and **Conversations** for social data results.

Once we select a result source, a list of all the related queries for that result source will be displayed. If we pick **Local SharePoint Results**, a sum of eighteen query rules will show.

Let's take the **Adobe PDF** query rule, as shown in the following screenshot, and discuss how it answers questions two and three stated in the previous section:

Adobe PDF		Advanced Query Text Match	Add Ranked Result Blocks
		Keywords: .pdf; pdf	PDFs for "{subjectTerms}"
		Advanced Query Text Match	
		Keywords: .pdf; pdf	
	10/16/2012	Result Type Commonly Clicked	
		Result Type: PDF	
		On Result Source	
		Local SharePoint Results	

The lighter block on the left-hand side answers the second question by listing all of the query conditions that will fire the query rule. The query rule will fire for any query that:

- Contains the keywords **pdf** or **.pdf** at the beginning of the query
- Contains the keywords **pdf** or **.pdf** at the end of the query
- A result type of PDF is commonly clicked for this specific query

Result Type Commonly Clicked is a special query condition that fires the query rule if other users in the system frequently clicked on a particular result type after they typed the same query.

The darker block on the right-hand side answers the last question. When the query rule fires, it will add a ranked result block for the matching results and set the title of **PDFs for "{subjectTerms}"** where the keyword **subjectTerms** represents the original search query the user typed.

Setting query conditions

In the previous section, we answered the first question and set the result source for the query. We also saw an example for query conditions that set the conditions a query rule will fire under.

When writing a query rule, you have six different types of query conditions to choose from. Some are quite self-explanatory (that is, Query Matches Keyword Exactly) while some need further attention.

Query Matches Dictionary Exactly

The Query Matches Dictionary Exactly query condition is almost identical to Query Matches Keyword Exactly, but instead of a free-text keyword, the rule will fire if a query matches a term from the specified taxonomy term set.

Query More Common in Source

This query condition will cause the query rule to fire if the query the user typed is more frequently used on a different result source than the one we are setting the query rule for.

For example, we create a query rule for the **Local SharePoint Results** result source and set the source of the **Query More Common in Source** rule to **Local Video Results**. If a user searches for Gameplay videos in the **Everything** search vertical with a query (which uses the **Local SharePoint Results** result source) and if that query has more frequently been used on the **Local Video Results** result source, the query rule will fire.

Result Type Commonly Clicked

This query condition will cause the query rule to fire if the query the user typed often ends up with users clicking on a result of a particular type.

For example, if a significant number of users who previously performed a search for Gameplay videos ended up clicking on a result of the type video, there is a big probability that the user is performing the search to look for a video result; so, we can provide it to him/her by showing a result block.

Advanced Query Text Match

This option allows us to type any regular expression we wish to create. Depending upon the condition, the query rule will fire.

When creating a query rule, we can combine all of these condition types and create a powerful rule that can react on the user's query even without the user explicitly telling us what he is looking for. An example of such a combined rule can be seen in the following screenshot:

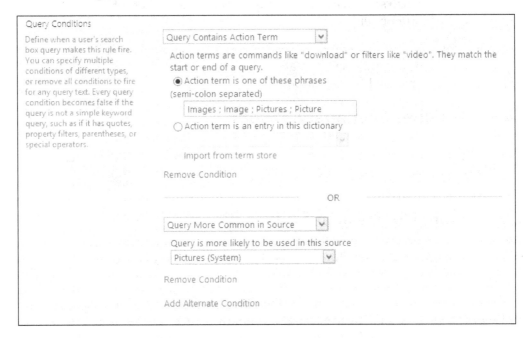

This query rule will fire if a query either contains one of the specified action terms or if the query is more commonly used in the pictures result source.

Setting the action

Now that we have defined under which result source the query rule is going to run and under what conditions, it's time to set what the query rule will actually do when it fires; and with this, we answer the third and final question.

We have three possible actions to choose from, and each represents a different type of action. Let's discuss these options now and gain an understanding of which action is best suitable for which given situation.

Promoted result

A promoted result is a result that appears on top of the results page. As we noted before, it is very similar to SharePoint 2010's best bet result.

Promoted results are most useful when you wish to promote one particular result and draw the user's attention to it. A promoted result doesn't have to be a textual link. When we create a promoted result, we can choose whether it will be displayed as a hyperlink (as shown in the beginning of the section) or as a banner as shown in the following screenshot:

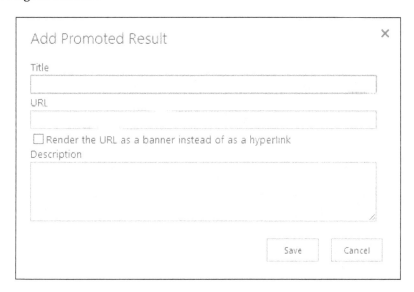

When the checkbox **Render the URL as a banner instead of as a hyperlink** is checked, SharePoint will render the hyperlink content inside of an iframe element, ignoring whatever you wrote in the **Title** and **Description** fields.

Result block

A result block is a selection of results that are displayed as a group and that are part of the core search results. What makes a result block stand out is the fact that the result it shows aren't necessarily coming from the local SharePoint index or from SharePoint.

When creating a result block, the two most basic settings we have to set are **Block Title** and **Query** as can be seen in the following screenshot:

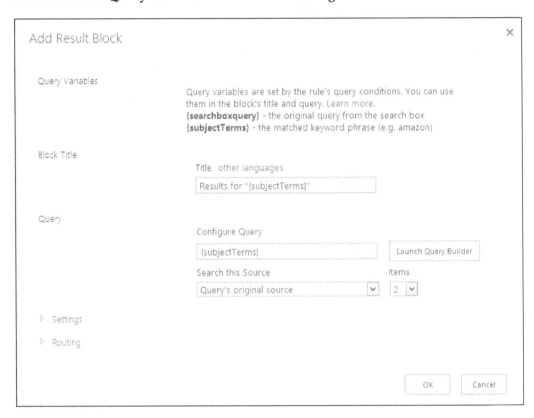

A query can be as simple as **{subjectTerms}**, which is the matched phrase from the user's query, or it can be a complex one including properties and calculations. We will discuss how to build queries in the next chapter, so for now we will use the default query.

In addition to the query, we can specify the source of the query. All the out of the box sources are available for use, along with any custom ones we will create.

The following are additional settings for a result block: whether or not to display a show more link, should the block be ranked or promoted, the display template (UI) of the block, and routing.

Change ranked results by changing the query

This action type is the most powerful one as it allows us to not only show or promote a given set of results but change the way the query is handled by SharePoint.

The query builder provides an easy way to either manipulate the query, to add additional keywords, to filter managed properties, or even to change result ranks using the **XRANK** keyword.

We will dive deep into the keyword query language and this action type in the next chapter.

Using the content search web part

When working with out of the box SharePoint search web parts, SharePoint 2013 simplifies the process by cutting down the number of web parts from 17 in SharePoint 2010 to just four.

In addition to the core search web parts, there are a number of new web parts that are powered by search. The most important of the bunch, without a doubt, is the content search web part.

The content search web part is the evolution of the content query web part from SharePoint 2007/2010. It allows us to display content straight from the search index, based on a query. For example, we can use the content search web part to display the latest document added on a specific site collection (that is, the knowledge center) to any other site collection in our farm using a simple query!

The content search web part infrastructure relies on two factors:

- A query built using the query builder
- A display template to render the results

We will discuss display the template in detail in *Chapter 4*, *Customizing the Look*, but for now, imagine display templates as HTML- and JavaScript-based template solutions for rendering results. Gone are the days of using code and XSLT for UI design.

When working with the content search web part, always keep its limitations at the back of your mind; they are as follows:

- The content the web part returns is only as fresh as the latest crawl. If you just uploaded a document and are searching for it, you won't find it.

- Only major versions of content are shown. Since the search index never crawls minor versions of content, this kind of content will not be shown using the content search web part.

- If a site is marked not to be indexed, the search content web part will not be able to query it; thus, it won't show any content from the site.

 At the time of writing the book, the content search web part is not available on Office 365. It is very likely that Microsoft will add it in a future update.

The content search web part has a few commonly used queries out of the box, such as recently changed items, items matching a tag, items matching a content type, and others. For example, we can easily set the content search web part to show all the latest discussions in a given site or show all of the latest videos on entire web applications. If we wish to create our own query, we can easily do so by switching to the advanced mode as shown in the following screenshot:

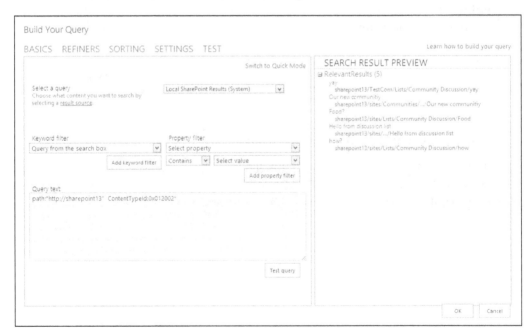

The query builder provides us with easy access to all of the managed properties and keyword filters, in addition to a preview box that shows the result of our query. The screenshot shows the query text for displaying all of the items of type discussion in a web application, whose URL is `http://sharepoint13`.

Don't get discouraged if you don't understand the query right away, we will dive deeper into the keyword query language in the next chapter.

Building a simple search-driven application

With all the theory we just discussed, it's time to put the wheels in motion. With the knowledge we gained so far in this chapter, we can build a simple search-driven application that will use query rules to react to users' intentions.

First, let's get our infrastructure in order and create two new sites as follows:

- A team site called `Video Games Center` that will host the content for our search-driven application
- A search center site that we will use to create the search logic on

Adding content

In order to show search results, we first need something to search for. Let's follow the ensuing steps to pour some content into our newly added team site:

1. Navigate to the newly added team site and add the following apps:
   - A picture library named `VideoGamesImages`
   - A document library named `VideoGamesDocuments`

   Once both the libraries have been created, rename them to `Video Games Center Images` and `Video Games Center Documents` respectively.

2. From the downloadable content of the book, unzip the `VideoGamesImages.rar` and `VideoGamesDocuments.rar` files and drag the files to the newly created picture library and document library respectively.

3. If you are using Office 365, wait for about 15 minutes before the continuous crawler picks up the new files. If you are using an on-premise installation, continue to the next step to perform an incremental crawl.

4. Head over to SharePoint's central admin and click on **Manage Service Applications**. Find your **Search Service Application** tab and click on it.

5. On the left-side menu, under the **Crawling category** click on **Content Sources**.

6. Locate the **Local SharePoint sites** content source, and using the little arrow on its right, click on **Start Incremental Crawl** as can be seen in the following screenshot:

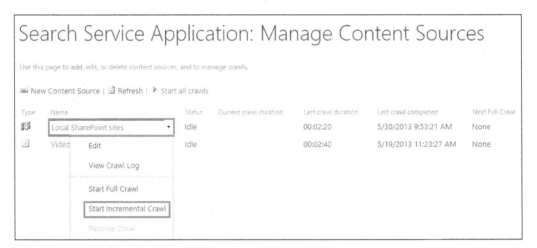

7. The status for the content source will change to **starting** and then **crawling**. Once the status returns to **Idle**, it means the crawl has finished and we can move on to the next section.

Creating the result source

As we noted before, the result source is the heart of a search-driven application. Follow these steps to create a result source called Video Games that will narrow the search to the two new libraries we just created:

1. Switch over to the search center site, then click on the cogwheel icon, and then click on **Site Settings**.

2. Under the **Search** category, click on **Result Sources**.

3. Click on the **New Result Source** button at the top of the page.

4. Name our new result source Video Games Results. Our result source queries a local SharePoint site (Video Games Center) and returns SharePoint results, so leave the default settings for **Protocol** and **Type**.

5. Now comes the interesting part. We wish to limit the query to only search inside the two new libraries we created. To achieve this goal, we will use the Keyword Query Language's site managed property that represents the SharePoint result's absolute URL.

6. The Keyword Query Language's syntax is quite simple: `<managed property name>:<value>`. We tell the search engine which managed property we wish to use, what operator to use (contains, equals to, and so on) on it, and what value to compare to. In our case, we are going to use `site:<your site url>/VideoGames*`.

7. The previous query will tell the search engine to look for content inside every library that contains the phrase "VideoGames" in its URL, under the specified site URL. In our environment, the query text will look as follows: `{searchTerms} site:hippodevssp.sharepoint.com/VideoGames*`.

8. To set the query, click on **Launch Query Builder** under **Query Transform** and add the new query as stated in the preceding steps (make sure to replace the site URL with your own). The page will look like the following screenshot:

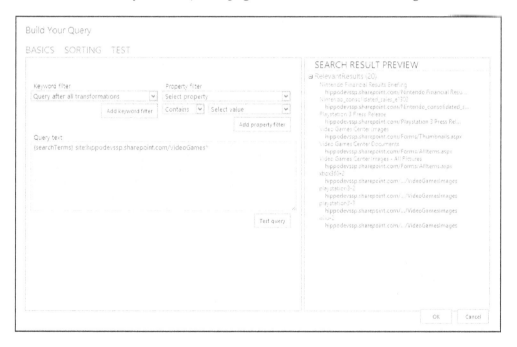

If everything went as expected, you should get a new preview of the affected results on the right-side of the window when clicking on the **Test query** button.

Click on the **OK** button to save the new query. Click on the **Save** button to save the result source.

Creating a search vertical

Now that we have the brain behind our new search-driven application, let's add the face as follows:

1. At the enterprise search center, click on the cogwheel icon and then click on **Add a page**.

2. Name the page anything you like and click on **OK**. This will create the landing page for the new search vertical.

3. Locate the **Search Results Web Part** button, click on the little arrow on its right, and choose **Edit Web Part**.

4. Click on the **Change Query** button. Above the button, we have the select query dropdown. Since this results page is dedicated to our result source, change the source in the dropdown to **Video Games Results** and click on **OK**. Publish the page.

5. The page will show all the results from both of our libraries. Now let's add a link to the new search vertical next to **Videos** so that it will be visible to users. Click on the cogwheel icon and then on **Site Settings**.

6. Under the **Search** section, click on **Search Settings**.

7. Scroll down to the **Configure Search Navigation** section of the page and click on **Add Link**. Give the new vertical a title of Video Games, and using the **Browse** button, browse to the page we created in step 2. Click on **OK** to save.

8. Navigate back to the search center site. Our new search vertical is proudly shown as in the following screenshot:

So far we've created the simplest of search-driven applications. We've created a new search vertical so users can search directly within the two asset libraries we've created. But now let's add a bit of logic to the application using search queries.

Adding a query rule

When we discussed query rules earlier in this chapter, we saw an example of a user searching for `xbox360 pictures` and getting back a result block showing images of an Xbox 360 console. Let's create this query rule now for our little application as follows:

1. Navigate to the search center, click on the cogwheel icon, and choose **Site Settings**.

2. Under the **Search** section, click on **Query Rules**.

3. The result source we wish to create the query rule for is our newly added **Video Games Results**. Select it using the first drop-down box (**Select a Result Source…**) and click on **New Query Rule**.

4. Name the rule `Images Rule`.

5. For the query conditions, select **Query Contains Action Term**. Make sure the first radio button (**Action term is one of these phrases**) is selected, and type `images ; image` in the text box. We consider `images` and `image` as actions because we do not want the search engine to look for <term> images or <term> image but for <term> only. The terms `images` and `image` act as a filter in this query.

6. The action we wish to perform is adding a result block; click on **Add Result Block**.

7. Change the block title to `{actionTerms} for "{subjectTerms}"` so users will know what they are looking at. Since both `{subjectTerms}` and `{actionTerms}` are placeholders, the title will actually be the action the user has searched for, followed by the term the user has searched for. For example, images for Xbox 360.

8. The query area is where we should direct most of our attention. We declared earlier that this result block should return only images. But images alone are not enough. We don't want it to just take any image from the picture library and show it. We want it to show pictures related to the search query the user typed. By setting the query to {subjectTerms} contenttype:picture, we are telling the search engine we wish to return results that match the query term (that is, Xbox 360), but also that we only want those results that have content of the type picture. Set the query as shown in the preceding part. Your **Edit Result Block** pop-up should look similar to the following screenshot:

9. Once the query is set, click on the **OK** button and then on **Save** to save the new query rule.

10. Navigate back to the search center and search for xbox360 images under the new **Video Games** search vertical. The expected outcome is as shown in the following screenshot:

Summary

This chapter mixed theory with practice. We started off by discussing result sources, the heart of search-driven applications. We saw examples on what result sources are, what they are used for, and got introduced to search verticals.

Query rules, the main concept of the chapter, was introduced next. Query rules are a new addition to SharePoint, and they allow us to respond intelligently to user queries. When building a query rule, you have to remember three questions: where is the user going to use this query rule (which search vertical)?, what makes this query rule fire?, and what does the query rule do once fired?

Once we understood the concept of query rules, we moved on and got introduced to the new king of search-related web parts: the content search web part.

The chapter ended with a step-by-step tutorial on creating a small and simple search-driven application based on the subjects discussed in this chapter.

While this search-driven application may seem simple, remember that it's only the beginning and that we will further enhance it down the road.

Take some time to familiarize yourself with query rules and try to create additional ones (for example, create a query rule that will detect if a certain query is more commonly used in the **Video Games Results** vertical than the **Everything** vertical and show results from that vertical in the result block). The more queries you create, the more you'll appreciate their power.

3
Using the New CSOM and RESTful APIs

SharePoint 2013 changes the way we, developers, extend the platform. In the previous versions, most, if not all, of the developing focus was on the server side. SharePoint 2013, however, changes this philosophy and puts the client side in the front seat. In this chapter, we will dive deep into the new client-side developing methods, get a better understanding of the choice of query language in SharePoint 2013 — **Keyword Query Language (KQL)**, and finish off with an introduction to the new developing model introduced in SharePoint 2013 — Apps.

In this chapter, we will cover the following topics:

- Introducing the Keyword Query Language
- Using the new client-side APIs
- Introducing to apps
- Building a SharePoint-hosted search-driven app

Understanding the Keyword Query Language

Whether users know it or not, every time they use SharePoint's search box, they are actually writing a keyword query. A keyword query consists of either a free text query, a **property restriction**, or both. In addition, keyword queries can include operators, such as OR, AND, and NOT.

The basics

A basic keyword query contains at least one search term (free text), and is case insensitive, which means that a search for xbox will return items containing both xbox and XBOX. Operators, on the other hand are case sensitive and must be written using uppercase letters, so searching for items containing either "xbox" or "playstation" will result in the following query: xbox OR playstation.

What if we wish to look for any item that begins with xbox and not just contains it? That's why we have the asterisk (*) operator. Searching for xbox* will return items such as xbox360, xbox720, and so on.

If we wish to look for items containing the exact phrase 'xbox 360', we put the phrase between quotes. If we just type xbox 360 without quotes, we will get items containing xbox and 360, but not necessarily the exact phrase "xbox 360". That means an item containing the phrase "A new xbox dashboard is available for download. Current 360 owners can get it right now" will be returned as a result, even though it has nothing to do with the phrase we searched for.

> Currently, keyword queries don't support suffix matching, which means we can't use the asterisk operator before a phrase, (that is, *xbox) only after (xbox*).

Property restrictions

Property restrictions help to narrow down the search results by adding conditions to the query that the results must meet in order to be shown to the user.

Property restrictions have a consistent syntax:

```
[Property Name] [Operator] [Property Value]
```

The property name is the name of the managed property we wish to filter by (that is, Author, Site, Created, and so on).

> Make sure the managed property you wish to filter by is set to Queryable. Setting a managed property to Queryable is done in the Search Schema page.

Property restriction supports several operators; each has its own purpose. The following operators are available:

Operator	Description
:	Restricts the search for results for which the specified property **contains** a specified value. An example would be `Author:Johnny`. The example will return all the items whose author name contains Johnny.
=	Restricts the search for results for which the specified property **equals** a specified value. An example would be `FileExtension=pptx`. The example will return all the items whose file type is PowerPoint and extension is `.pptx`.
<>	Restricts the search for results for which the specified property is **not equal** to a specified value. An example would be `Path<>http://sharepoint`. The example will return all the items whose path isn't `http://sharepoint`.
> / >=	Restricts the search for results for which the specified property is **greater than** / **greater than or equal** to the specified value. An example would be `Created>=24/4/2013`. The example will return all the items that were created on or after April 24, 2013.
< / =<	Restricts the search for results for which the specified property is less than / less than or equal to the specified value. An example would be `Created<=24/4/2013`. The example will return all the items that were created on or before April 24, 2013.
value1...value2	Restricts the search for results for which the specified property **falls between** a specified range. An example would be `Created=1/4/2013...30/4/2013`. The example will return all the items that were created between the 1st and the 30th of April, 2013.

What gives keyword query its true power is the ability to combine property restrictions together. Say, we wish to find all the documents containing the word `Console` and authored by someone named `Ben`. Our query will look as follows:

```
Console AND IsDocument:1 AND Author:Ben
```

What about all the Excel files containing the exact phrase "quarterly report", authored between the January 1 and the March 30 and hosted on either the finance department's intranet located at `http://sharepoint/sites/finance` or the management's intranet at `http://sharepoint/management`? It may sound quite complicated but the query will end up looking like the following:

```
"quarterly report" AND FileExtension=xlsx AND
   LastModifiedTime=1/1/2013...30/3/2013 AND
      (path:http://sharepoint/finance OR
        path:http://sharepoint/management)
```

By combining different managed properties and property restrictions, we can be as specific or as open as we wish regarding our results.

XRANK

A special kind of property restriction is the XRANK property. XRANK is used to boost results at query time based on a specific rule. Changing the results relevance on the fly is an extremely powerful feature as it enables us to easily promote certain results dynamically.

Say the HR department of our company wishes that if someone searches for a term that is in their taxonomy term store (for example, Vacation), we will boost any result that is a Word file. Using XRANK, our query will look as follows:

```
{searchTerm} XRANK(cb=1000) FileExtension=docx
```

The query searches for whatever the search term is and gives a constant boost (cb) of 1000 points to any result that has a file extension of .docx.

Constant boost (or cb) is just one of the available parameters XRANK can handle. Other parameters include normalized boost (nb), range boost (rb), or percentage boost (pb).

We will use XRANK later in the book. If you wish to dive deeper into XRANK, visit the MSDN documentation about XRANK at `http://msdn.microsoft.com/en-us/library/ee558911.aspx`.

Synonyms

In some cases we wish to search for a term that has a synonym. Using the `Words` operator, we can specify synonyms and return results that match either of the specified terms. The `Words` operator can be used with free text expressions only, and it is not supported in property restrictions.

Say we wish to find results that contain either `Phone` or `Telephone`. What would be the difference between using `Words(Phone,Telephone)` and `Phone OR Telephone`?

The answer is simply the rank. When using the `Words` operator, both `Phone` and `Telephone` are treated as synonyms and not separate terms. Therefore, any instance of these words is ranked as if they were the same term. An item containing the term `Phone` three times and the term `Telephone` two times will rank the same as an item containing only the term `Phone` five times.

Using the `OR` operator means that each term is ranked on its own. An item with three instances of `Phone` and two instances of `Telephone` will be ranked higher than an item containing only `Phone` five times. `OR` ranks the terms as separate terms, and as such each has its own ranking.

Using the new client-side APIs

For the first time in SharePoint history, Microsoft treats client-side developing as a first-class citizen in SharePoint. With a set of RESTful APIs that provide access to almost every aspect of SharePoint and a redesigned client-side object model, we, SharePoint developers, can create powerful and engaging client-side applications.

`Search`, which is a major element in SharePoint 2013, embraces the new methodology and enables us to develop search-driven applications using JavaScript and managed code (C#).

Before we go ahead and discuss the usage of the new client-side APIs, let's dive into what these APIs are.

RESTful API

REST (or Representational State Transfer) is a simple alternative to **SOAP** (or Simple Object Access Protocol) based on an HTTP request/response pair. To communicate with a REST service, the client sends an HTTP request using a unique URI (Unique Resource Identifier).

REST and SharePoint 2013

SharePoint 2013's REST API allows us to perform **CRUD** (**Create**, **Read**, **Update**, and **Delete**) operations on most of SharePoint's client object model types and members using standard HTTP verbs. Reading content using REST is done using the `GET` verb, inserting items is done using `POST`, `PUT` is used for updating content, and `Delete`, big surprise here, is used for deleting content.

By default, SharePoint uses the **ATOM** (XML) protocol to respond to REST calls, but if we are planning on using a JavaScript framework such as jQuery, we would much rather work with JSON objects. Changing the response protocol for a REST call is done by sending an `Accept` header to the REST service with the desired format. The `Accept` header is sent on a per-call basis.

Using REST is as easy as typing a URL in the browser's address bar. Most of SharePoint's REST calls are structured using the following syntax:

```
http://servername/site/_api/<namespace>/object/parameters/?$OData
```

The namespace is the main entry point for the REST call. The possible values for an entry point are as follows:

- **Site**: This value corresponds to `SPContext.Current.Site` in SharePoint's object model.
- **Web**: This value corresponds to `SPContext.Current.Web` in SharePoint's object model.
- **SP.UserProfiles.PeopleManager**: This value represents the user profile manager and enables us to work with social-related content.
- **Search**: This value is the jewel in the crown. It represents the search engine and enables us to work with search-related content.
- **Publishing**: This value represents the publishing features of SharePoint 2013.

Once the namespace is set, it's time to specify an object. `Object`, just like in SharePoint's object model, represents a SharePoint item, for example, `List`. To get the entire collection of lists under the current site, the following syntax is used:

```
http://servername/site/_api/web/lists
```

When we wish to target just a specific object (that is, a list), we use parameters. An example for such a parameter is `getbytitle`. Using a parameter is as easy as the following syntax:

```
http://servername/site/_api/web/lists/getbytitle('Reports')
```

The preceding syntax will return all the items of a list named `Reports`.

What makes REST so unique is its ability to use OData query operators to filter results. OData supports many query operators, and a complete list in the MSDN documentation can be found at `http://msdn.microsoft.com/en-us/library/sharepoint/fp142385(v=office.15).aspx`.

A common use for query operators is returning a specific number of rows from a list. The following syntax returns the top 10 rows from a list called `Reports`:

```
http://servername/site/_api/web/lists/getbytitle('Reports')/
items$top=10
```

And what if we wish to return a set of 10 results, starting from row 10? We use the `$skip` operator:

```
http://servername/site/_api/web/lists/getbytitle('Reports')/
items$skip=10$top=10
```

Using REST

As fun as writing REST in a browser's address bar is, it's not really a useful method. In most cases, we will find ourselves using REST in a JavaScript app. The easiest way to use REST with JavaScript is by using jQuery's `$.ajax` and `$.getjson` methods. Calling the preceding query using jQuery is done using the following code:

```
var restUrl =
  "http://hippodevssp.sharepoint.com/sites/VideoGames/web/lists/
getbytitle('Reports')/items$top=10";
$.getJSON(restUrl, function (data) {
    /* do something useful with the data here */
});
```

> We mentioned earlier that in order to work with JSON objects, we must add an `Accept` header telling SharePoint we wish to get a JSON response. Adding the `Accept` header in jQuery is done using the following code:
>
> ```
> $.ajaxSetup({
>     'beforeSend': function (xhr) {
>     xhr.setRequestHeader("ACCEPT",
>     "application/json;odata=verbose");
>     }
> });
> ```

As its name implies, `$.getjson` is only good for GET requests. If we wish to create a POST request, we will use the `$.ajax` method.

Adding a new item to the `Reports` list is done using the following code:

```
$.ajax({
  url: "http://servername/site/_api/web/lists/getbytitle('Reports')/
items",
  method: "POST",
  data: JSON.stringify({ '__metadata': { 'type':
    'SP.Data.ReportsListItem' }, 'Title': 'New item!'}),
  headers: {
    "X-RequestDigest": $("#__REQUESTDIGEST").val()
```

```
      "accept": "application/json;odata=verbose"
      "content-type": "application/json;odata=verbose"
    },
    success: function () { alert("Success!") },
    error: function (xhr, ajaxOptions, thrownError) {
      alert("POST error:\n" + xhr.status + "\n" + thrownError);
    }
  });
```

Downloading the example code

You can download the example code files for all Packt books you have purchased from your account at http://www. packtpub.com. If you purchased this book elsewhere, you can visit http://www.packtpub.com/support and register to have the files e-mailed directly to you

A few things to notice in this REST call are as follows:

- The method property is set to POST as we are posting data back to SharePoint.
- The data property has a predefined syntax; the __metadata JSON object has its type always set to SP.Data.<List name>ListItem. In our case its SP.Data.ReportsListItem. After the Type object, we can write all the columns we wish to have on our new item.
- Make sure to add success and error callbacks. When things go the other way, you will want to know what failed.

While not as common as jQuery, we can use REST with C# code as well. The following code shows how to call REST using C# to read the items of the Reports list:

```
HttpWebRequest listRESTRequest =
  (HttpWebRequest)HttpWebRequest.Create("http://
hippodevssp.sharepoint.com/sites/videogames/_api/Web/lists/
getbytitle('Reports')");
listRESTRequest.Method = "GET";
listRESTRequest.Accept = "application/atom+xml";
listRESTRequest.ContentType = "application/atom+xml;type=entry";
HttpWebResponse listRESTResponse =
  (HttpWebResponse)listRESTRequest.GetResponse();

StreamReader listReader = new
  StreamReader(listRESTResponse.GetResponseStream());
var listXml = new XmlDocument();
listXml.LoadXml(listReader.ReadToEnd());
```

To make things a little bit easier, you can use the great open source project RESTSharp (http://restsharp.org/) to make REST calls in C#.

REST and search

Now that we understand what REST is and how to use it, let's see how we can relate it to search. The entry point for search is, big surprise, search. Under the search namespace we have the following objects:

- query: This object performs a query against the search engine and retrieves results.

- postquery: This object same as query, but allows the use of POST instead of GET in order to overcome possible URL length restrictions.

- suggest: This object used to get query suggestions. Can only be used with GET.

To perform a search, we use the query object with the querytext parameter, as follows:

```
http://servername/site/_api/search/query?querytext='Xbox 360'
```

Making this REST call on our **Video Games** site will result as follows:

```
"__metadata": {
  "type": "SP.KeyValue"
},
  "Key": "Rank",
  "Value": "11.5442914962769",
  "ValueType": "Edm.Double"
}, {
"__metadata": {
  "type": "SP.KeyValue"
},
  "Key": "DocId",
  "Value": "27972637",
  "ValueType": "Edm.Int64"
}, {
"__metadata": {
  "type": "SP.KeyValue"
},
  "Key": "WorkId",
  "Value": "27972637",
  "ValueType": "Edm.Int64"
}, {
"__metadata": {
  "type": "SP.KeyValue"
  },
  "Key": "Title",
  "Value": "Video Games Center Images",
  "ValueType": "Edm.String"
}, {
```

```
"__metadata": {
  "type": "SP.KeyValue"
},
  "Key": "Author",
  "Value": "Johnny Tordgeman",
  "ValueType": "Edm.String"
}, {
...
```

Now that's a lot of JSON for just one result! When we use the REST API to perform a search query, we get back all the information about that result. This information includes the author, the result's rank, its title, and much more.

An equally important parameter of the `Query` namespace is `sourceid`. In the previous chapter, we declared a result source called **Video Games Results**, which narrows the query to only look for results in the predefined libraries. If we wish to use that result source with our REST call, we append the `sourceid` parameter. The `sourceid` parameter specifies the **Globally Unique Identifier** (**GUID**) of the result source we wish to use. Searching for `xbox360` within our **Video Games Results** result source will look as follows:

```
https://servername/site/_api/search/query?querytext='xbox360'&sourceid
='9cdd3749-4930-4c8c-a911-99ba652b157a'
```

You may be asking yourself "where do I get the result source's unique identifier from?" The answer is quite simple. When you click on a result source, look at the end of the address bar. You'll find the source ID there as shown highlighted in the following screenshot:

When we wish to limit the number of results returned or wish to start at a specified result index, we use the `startrow` and `rowlimit` parameters. The former is a zero-based index specifying the first result that should be returned. The latter specifies the maximum number of results that the search engine will return. For example, if we wish to get a maximum of five results, starting from the 10th result, we will use the following syntax:

```
https://servername/site/_api/search/query?querytext='xbox360'&sourceid
='9cdd3749-4930-4c8c-a911-99ba652b157a'&startrow=9&rowlimit=5
```

As we can see, each result item we get back has its full list of properties returned. What if we only need one or two properties? We shouldn't waste bandwidth and return all of the properties. This is when the `selectproperties` parameter should be used. This parameter accepts a list of parameters that should be returned for each result. If we wish to return only the `Author` and `Title` parameters for example, we will use the following syntax:

```
https://servername/site/_api/search/query?querytext='xbox360'&sourcei
d='9cdd3749-4930-4c8c-a911-99ba652b157a'&selectproperties='Title,Auth
or'
```

To get results in a specified language, we can set the `culture` parameter. It specifies an LCID (Locale ID) representing the requested language. If we wish to return results only in the `English` language, we will use the following syntax:

```
https://servername/site/_api/search/query?querytext='xbox360'&sourceid
='9cdd3749-4930-4c8c-a911-99ba652b157a'&selectproperties='Title,Author
'&culture=1033
```

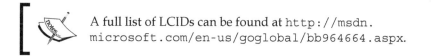 A full list of LCIDs can be found at `http://msdn.microsoft.com/en-us/goglobal/bb964664.aspx`.

There are many more properties we can use for a search REST call. If you wish to go deeper, check out Search Space's post on the SharePoint 2013 Search REST API at `http://blogs.msdn.com/b/nadeemis/archive/2012/08/24/sharepoint-2013-search-rest-api.aspx`.

Client Side Object Model (CSOM)

Other than REST, SharePoint 2013 introduces a revamped client object model. The client object model was first introduced in SharePoint 2010 and provided a way for developers to interact with SharePoint using one of three methods:

- **Managed code**: Using C#
- **Managed code**: Using Silverlight
- **Unmanaged Code**: Using JavaScript

Since CSOM is not new to SharePoint 2013, we will not focus on how to work with it for the remainder of the chapter. If you need a refresh, or wish to understand how to perform basic operations with CSOM, head over to the MSDN documentation at `http://msdn.microsoft.com/en-us/library/fp179912.aspx`.

For the remainder of the chapter, we will focus on the JavaScript variant and the `search` object.

CSOM and search

The entry point for search in CSOM is the `KeywordQuery` class, which is under the `Microsoft.SharePoint.Client.Search.Query` namespace. The process of sending a query to the engine and getting back results using CSOM is as follows:

1. We initiate the `KeywordQuery` class and use its `set_queryText` method to set the search query.

2. We initiate the `SearchExecuter` class and use its `executeQuery` method to tell the client context object to perform the search once executed.

3. We execute the client context object using its `executeQueryAsync` method. If the request succeeded, the success callback will be called.

The preceding steps result in the following code when trying to search for `xbox360`:

```
var context = SP.ClientContext.get_current();
var keywordQuery = new
  Microsoft.SharePoint.Client.Search.Query.KeywordQuery(context);
keywordQuery.set_queryText("xbox360");
var searchExecutor = new
  Microsoft.SharePoint.Client.Search.Query.SearchExecutor(context);
results = searchExecutor.executeQuery(keywordQuery);
context.executeQueryAsync(onQuerySuccess, onQueryFailed);
```

The `ResultRows` array is the result of successfully executing the query. We can iterate through the array using jQuery's `$.each` method and print the results to the user however we like. It is recommended we use some templating engine such as jsRender or Handlebars to easily create the graphic representation of the results.

Other than `set_queryText`, the `KeywordQuery` object holds everything we discussed earlier on the REST API section. Setting the result source ID is done using the `set_sourceId` method, the culture is set using the `set_culture` method, and so on.

A common place to use either the REST API or the JavaScript CSOM is an app, which is what we are going to discuss next.

An app in SharePoint 2013 is a new development model introduced in SharePoint 2013. The easiest way to explain what apps are is to compare it to the mobile world. Think about apps for your smartphone. An app is a piece of software that you install on your mobile OS from a marketplace or installation files (that is, `.apk` for Android). Prior to the installation, the app tells you all the permissions it needs in order to run, and you can choose whether to install it or not. Apps for SharePoint are almost identical.

In a nutshell, apps are the evolution of SharePoint 2010's sandbox solutions. Sandbox solutions were never a big hit in the SharePoint community as they had a lot of limitations. One of the biggest limitations was that sandbox solutions couldn't make calls to external web services. Apps tackle many of those limitations and present a nice and lean client-based development model.

An app uses standard web technologies such as HTML and JavaScript. In some cases, apps may use **OAuth authentication** as well. Just like mobile OS apps, SharePoint apps also declare permission requests before they are installed, and the site owner can choose whether to install an app or not. The following screenshot shows an app request for access permissions:

Apps have three hosting options; each is used for different scenarios.

A SharePoint-hosted app

A SharePoint-hosted App is basically an app that runs in the context of SharePoint. SharePoint-hosted apps can only use client-side code to implement behavior and UX (User Experience). A SharePoint-hosted app runs in an isolated sub website, which is created during its installation, and as such, SharePoint-hosted apps do not require any special authentication method.

A provider hosted app

A provider hosted app is an app that runs in any environment we choose and written in any language we choose. It is up to us, the app developers, to supply the hosting infrastructure, which can either be a local server or a cloud-based provider such as Amazon. It is not recommended to use Windows Azure as an infrastructure for provider hosted apps, as Azure has its own hosting option for apps. Communication with SharePoint is done using CSOM and REST calls with OAuth authentication through **ACS (Azure Access Services)**.

An autohosted app

Autohosted apps are apps that are hosted on Windows Azure, and can make use of Azure SQL for database purposes. Once installed, the app's web deployment manifest creates a new Azure web service instance and an optional SQL database instance. Just like provider hosted apps, autohosted apps communicate with SharePoint using CSOM and REST and OAuth authentication.

Both autohosted and provider hosted methods enable us to write feature-rich apps with code behind, without deploying anything to SharePoint. That helps to keep our SharePoint installation more intact. SharePoint-hosted apps are client-side-based apps, which are deployed on SharePoint, and as such cannot have any server-side code.

Regardless of which deployment option you choose, when an app is installed to a SharePoint instance and added on a page, SharePoint basically adds an iframe element, which displays the app's entrance page. Always keep in mind that apps are isolated from the SharePoint runtime. Every time an app is executed, SharePoint generates a new app domain with a unique URL.

Publishing an app

Once our app is developed we want users to, well, use it. Publishing an app makes it available to users. There are two places we can publish an app to:

- **The Office Store**: The Office Store is the public app catalogue for Office applications. Everyone can access the store and acquire free or paid apps. The Office Store supports all of the deployment models mentioned previously. The Office Store, as shown in the following screenshot, looks like any other marketplace you may know from the mobile world:

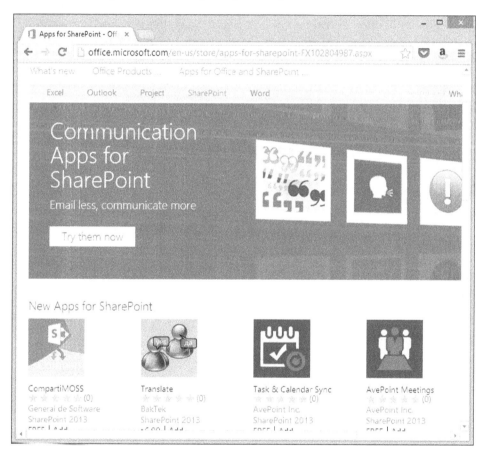

- **An internal organization app catalogue**: On-premise, SharePoint installation and Office 365 tenants have a local organizational catalog where SharePoint developers can develop apps for internal use only. No one outside the organization can access these apps. Just like the Office Store, all the deployment models are supported for the internal catalog.

Publishing an app to the Office Store requires you to register as a developer and fill out tax-related forms. If you are interested in publishing apps, check out the MSDN guide at `http://msdn.microsoft.com/en-us/library/jj220037.aspx`.

Apps can fill out an entire book (and actually have), and in our search-related book we won't go any deeper. If you feel like you wish to go deeper (and you should), check out *Microsoft SharePoint 2013 App Development, Scot Hillier and Ted Pattison, Microsoft Press*.

In the next section, we are going to build a SharePoint-hosted search-driven app that uses both REST and CSOM to access the search engine.

Building a SharePoint-hosted search-driven app

Now that we know how to use the new client-side APIs, how keyword queries work, and the overall idea of apps, let's combine all that knowledge and create a client-side search-driven app.

We mentioned in the previous chapter that the Content Search Web Part is not available in Office 365. What we will build now is a simple content search like web part that will aggregate all the tasks a user has over the entire tenant.

The end result of this section is as follows:

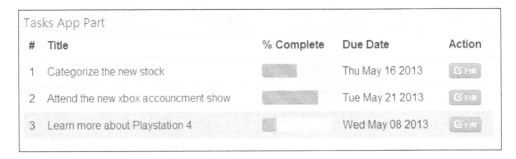

Create task apps (lists)

Create a task app (list) on the **Video Games** site, and any other sites you may have. Add some tasks that are assigned to your user and other users and wait a bit for the continuous crawl to pick up the new content.

Understanding the requirements

Our requirements are to display all the tasks from everywhere in the tenant for a specific user. Naturally, you may think that creating a result source is the first step in creating this app. Think about it a bit harder: when we created a result source earlier, we created it on the **Search** site because the search happened on the search site. Now, the search can happen on any site (wherever the site admin places our app part) and should search any site.

So what should we do? We should simply query the **Local SharePoint Results** source (which is the default one) with a query that uses property restriction. The two properties we wish to restrict are:

- A content type of `Task`
- An `AssignedTo` value of the user who performs the query

The resulting query of these property restrictions is as follows:

```
ContentType=Task AND AssignedTo='{username}'
```

Now we face another problem. How can we tell at runtime who the current user is? Well, it's quite simple actually. You'll find out momentarily when we start building our app.

Building the app

To get started, open the **TasksApp-Starter** project from the downloadable content of the book.

The first task we shall complete is to get the current user's display name. We will do that by using the JavaScript Client Object Model. Open the `App.js` file located under the `Scripts` folder. Currently it consists of a single line that initiates the client context. The easiest way to get the current user would be to use the `get_currentUser` method of the CSOM's web object. Add the following code snippet right after the context initiation line:

```
var user = context.get_web().get_currentUser();
```

`context.get_web` will take care of getting the currently used web, while `get_currentUser` will take care of getting the current user object.

In addition, we will need one global variable: `appWebUrl`. The variable will hold the URL of the app itself. Add the following snippet following the previously added code:

```
var appWebUrl;
```

Next, let's perform some initializations, which our app needs. Add the following code snippet to `app.js`:

```
$(document).ready(function () {
  appWebUrl =
  decodeURIComponent(getQueryStringParameter("SPAppWebUrl"));

  $.ajaxSetup({
    'beforeSend': function (xhr) {
      xhr.setRequestHeader("ACCEPT",
      "application/json;odata=verbose");
    }
  });

  context.load(user);
  context.executeQueryAsync(onGetUserSuccess, onGetUserFail);
});
```

The code handles the following:

- Sets the `appWebUrl` variable to the query string value of `SPAppWebUrl`, which represents the app subweb URL. It is the dynamic address the app was assigned during its creation.
- Adds an accept header to all outgoing Ajax calls from jQuery. This step is required in order to get back JSON objects from SharePoint's REST API.
- Loads and executes the current user object we initiated earlier. If the call to get the user is successful, the `onGetUserSuccess` delegate is called; otherwise the `onGetUserFail` delegate is called.

The `onGetUserFail` method is quite simple. Its entire purpose in life is to alert the user that an error has occurred. Its implementation is as follows:

```
function onGetUserFail(sender, args) {
  alert("Something went wrong: " + args.get_errorDetails());
}
```

The `onGetUserSuccess` method is the heart of our application. This method calls the REST API and gets back the data that we will display to the user. The method implementation is as follows:

```
function onGetUserSucces() {
  var restURL = appWebUrl +
  "/_api/search/query?querytext='ContentType=Task AND
  AssignedTo=\"" + user.get_title() +
  "\"'&selectproperties='Title,Author,PercentCompleteOWSNMBR,DueDateO
WSDATE,Path'";
  $.getJSON(restURL, function (data) {
  SetTasksUI(data.d.query.PrimaryQueryResult.RelevantResults.Table.
Rows);
  });
}
```

The query consists of the property restrictions we discussed previously, and a set of selected properties that we will use in our app. If we didn't specify which properties we wanted, we would have got back 42(!) properties, and that's, in most cases, a waste of bandwidth.

Once the `getJSON` method gets data back from SharePoint, we send it to the `SetTaskUI` method. All the results that the REST API returns are located under the `data.d.query` namespace, and `Rows` is the collection of the `results` objects.

The `SetTaskUI` method takes the `results` array and builds the HTML showing it using the `$.each` method for iterating through the `results` array. The method's implementation is as follows:

```
function SetTasksUI(dataRows) {
  var htmlRows = "";
  $.each(dataRows.results, function (index, item) {
    var title = $.grep(item.Cells.results, function (e) {
      return e.Key == "Title"; });
    var perComplete = parseInt($.grep(item.Cells.results, function
      (e) { return e.Key == "PercentCompleteOWSNMBR";
        })[0].Value*100);
    var dueDate = new Date($.grep(item.Cells.results, function (e)
      { return e.Key == "DueDateOWSDATE"; })[0].Value);
    var path = $.grep(item.Cells.results, function (e) { return
      e.Key == "Path"; })[0].Value;

    var className = dueDate > new Date() ? "regular" : "error";
```

```
        htmlRows += "<tr class='" + className + "'><td>"
          +parseInt(index + 1) + "</td><td><div class='titleDiv'><a
            target='_blank' href='" + path + "'>" + title[0].Value +
             "</a></div></td><td><div class='progress progress-success
              progress-striped'><div class='bar' style='width: "
                +perComplete + "%'></div></div></td><td>"
                  +dueDate.toDateString() + "</td><td><div class='btn
                    btn-mini btn-warning'><i class='icon-edit icon-
                       white'></i>Edit</div></td></tr>";

    });
    $(".table").append(htmlRows);
    $(".btn-warning").on("click", function () {

    });

    $(".loader").fadeOut(function () {
      $(".content").fadeIn();
    });
}
```

Each result in the `results` array is an object that has a key and a value. Using the `$.grep` method, we can get an object's value by comparing an object property (in our case, the key) to a specified value.

If you debug the app right now, you'll notice that you don't get any `results` back. The reason for that is not that our query was incorrect or that we used the wrong content type. The reason for that is we didn't request for the app's permission to access the search engine.

To request the search permission click on the `AppManifest.xml` file, and under the **Permissions** tab set the scope to **Search** and the permission to **QueryAsUserIgnoreAppPrincipal**. Once set, your permission tab should look as follows:

General	Permissions	Prerequisites	Supported Locales	Remote Endpoints

Specify the permissions that your app for SharePoint will request from the user at installation time.

☐ Allow the app to make app-only calls to SharePoint. Learn more about app authentication policy.

Scope	Permission	Properties
Search	QueryAsUserIgnoreAppPrinci	

Run the app again and you should get a result similar to the following screenshot:

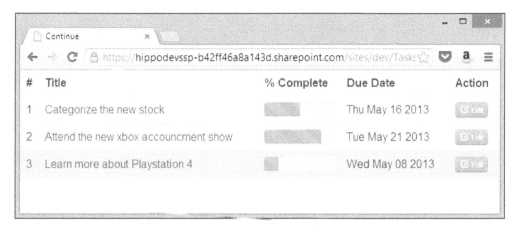

We haven't implemented the **Edit** button as it's not really search related. If you are interested in seeing the full implementation, it will be posted on the author's blog at `http://blog.johnnyt.me`.

Summary

This chapter covered a lot in terms of client-side developing. We started with deep diving into the Keyword Query Language, and understood how to query the search engine and get only the results and properties we wanted. We moved on to discussing the new client APIs that SharePoint 2013 introduces: REST and CSOM. We saw the differences between the two methods, use cases, and properties for both. Next, we briefly discussed the concept of apps, the new development model introduced in SharePoint 2013.

The chapter ended with a step-by-step tutorial on creating a client-side-based SharePoint-hosted search-driven app based on the subjects discussed in this chapter. In the next chapter we are going to deal with customizing the results' appearance. Using result types and display templates, which are the two new concepts introduced in SharePoint 2013, we can give each result type a unique appearance. So get your artistic nature ready and head over to the next chapter.

4
Customizing the Look

So far we dealt with the logic behind search results: how to get them, how to show only certain results, how to boost results, and so on. We have, however, relied on the core presentation of SharePoint to display the results. In this chapter we are going to focus on how to change the presentation of results. SharePoint 2013 introduced new concepts called result types and display templates, which, by using standard web technologies, help us achieve the look we are after.

In this chapter, we will cover the following topics:

- Working with result types
- Building a design template

Result types and design templates

Both result types and design templates are new concepts introduced in SharePoint 2013. Kate Dramstad, a program manager from the SharePoint search team at Microsoft, describes both concepts in a single, easy-to-remember formula: *result types + design templates = rich search experience.*

When we perform a search we get back results. Some results are documents, others are pictures, SharePoint items, or just about anything else. Up until SharePoint 2010, all results, no matter which type they were, looked quite the same. Take a look at the following screenshot showing a results page from FAST for SharePoint 2010:

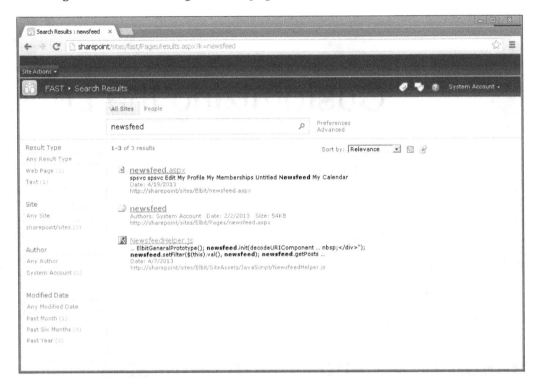

The results are dull looking, can't be told apart, and in order to find what you are looking for, you have to scan the results up and down with your eyes and zero in on your desired result.

Now let's look at how results are displayed in SharePoint 2013:

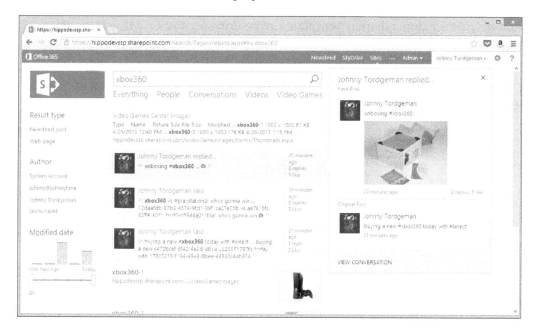

What a difference! The page looks much more alive and vibrant, with easy distinguishing of different result types and a whole new hover panel, which provides information about the hovered item and is completely customizable.

Display templates

Search, and its related web parts, makes heavy use of display templates instead of plain old **XSLT (Extensible Stylesheet Language Transformations)**. Display templates are basically snippets of HTML and JavaScript, which control the appearance and behavior of search results. SharePoint ships with a bunch of display templates that we can use out of the box, but we can also create our own custom ones.

Similar to master pages, it is recommended to copy an existing display template that is close in nature to what we strive to achieve and start our customization from it. Customizing a display template can be done on any HTML editor, or if you choose, even Notepad. Once we upload the HTML template, SharePoint takes care of creating the companion JavaScript file all by itself.

If we tear apart the results page, we can distinguish four different layers of display templates:

The layers are as follows:

- **Filters layer**: In the preceding screenshot they are highlighted with the green border on the left and numbered 1. This layer shows the new refinement panel area that is not limited to text alone, but also enables the use of UX elements such as sliders, sliders with graphs, and so on.

- **Control layer**: In the preceding screenshot they are highlighted with the red border in the middle and numbered 2. This layer shows that not only results but also controls can be templated. We will see what a templated control looks like later in the chapter.

- **Item layer**: In the preceding screenshot they are highlighted with the orange border in the middle and numbered 3. This layer shows that each result type can be templated to look unique. For example, in the screenshot we see how a site result (the first result), conversation results (next three results), and image result (last one) looks like. Each result type has its own display template.

- **Hover panel layer**: In the preceding screenshot, they are highlighted with the blue border on the right and numbered 4. They are introduced in SharePoint 2013, the hover panel shows information on a hovered result. The extra information can be a preview of the document (using Office Web Apps), a bigger version of an image or just about anything we like, as we can template the hover panel just like any other layer.

 Display templates are stored in a site's master page gallery under the `Display templates` folder.

Each one of these layers is controlled by display templates. But if design templates are the beauty, what are the brains? Well, that is result types.

Result types

Result types are the glue between design templates (UX—user experience) and the type of search result they template. You can think of result types as the brain behind the templating engine.

Using result types enables administrators to create display templates to be displayed based upon the type of content that is returned from the search engine. Each result type is defined by a rule and is bound to a result source. In addition, each result type is associated with a single display template.

Just like display templates, SharePoint ships with it a set of out of the box result types that match popular content. For example, SharePoint renders Word document results using the `Item_Word.html` display templates within any result source if the item matches the Microsoft Word type of content. However, if an item matches the PDF type of content, the result will be rendered using the `Item_PDF.html` display template.

Defining a result type is a process much like creating a query rule. We will create our first result type and display template towards the end of the chapter.

Both result types and display templates are used not only for search results, but also for other web parts as well, such as the Content Search Web Part.

Styling results in a Content Search Web Part

The **Content Search Web Part (CSWP)** comes in handy when we wish to show search-driven content to users quickly and without any interaction on their side.

When adding a CSWP we have two sections to set: **Search Criteria** and **Display Templates**. Each section has its unique settings, explained as follows:

1. The search criteria section is equivalent to the result type. Using the Query Builder we tell the web part which result type it should get. The Query Builder enables us to either choose one of the built-in queries (latest documents, items related to current user, and so on) or build our own. In addition, we can set the scope of the search. It can either be the current site, current site collection, or a URL. For our example, we will set the query to be **Documents(System)**, meaning it searches for the latest documents, and the scope to **Current site collection**:

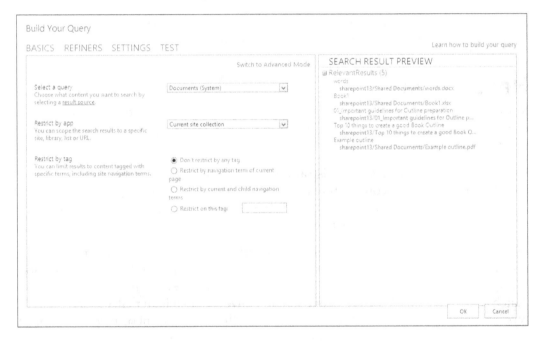

2. Next, we set the display template for the control holding the results. This is equivalent to the Control layer we mentioned earlier. The CSWP provides three control templates: **List**, **List with Paging**, and **Slideshow**. The control templates change the way the container of the items looks. To compare the different templates, take a look at how the container looks when the **List** template is chosen:

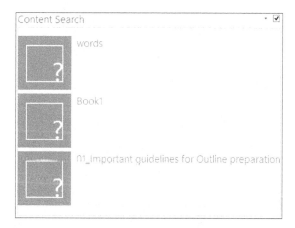

3. And the following screenshot displays how the exact same list looks when the **Slideshow** template is chosen:

Since our content is not images, rendering the control as **Slideshow** makes no sense.

4. Last but not least, we set the **Item** display template. As usual, SharePoint comes with a set of built-in item templates, each designated for different item types. By default, the **Picture on left, 3 lines on right** item display template is selected. By looking at the preceding screenshot we can see it's not right for our results. Since we are searching for documents, we don't have a picture representing them so the left area looks quite dull. If we change the **Item** display template to **Two lines** we will get a much more suitable result:

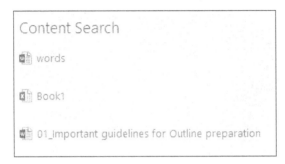

Display templates allow us to change the look of our results instantly. While playing around with the out-of-the-box display templates is fun, extending them is even better. If you look at the **Two lines** template that we chose for the CSWP, it seems kind of empty. All we have is the document type, represented by an icon, and the name of the document. Let's extend this display template and add the last modified date and the author of the document to the display.

Creating a custom display template

As we mentioned earlier, the best way to extend a display template is to copy and paste a template that is close in nature to what we wish to achieve, and customize it. So, as we wish to extend the **Two lines** template, open SharePoint Designer, navigate to **Master Page Gallery** | **Display Templates** | **Content Web Parts** of the site you previously added the CSWP, and copy and paste the Item_TwoLines.html file into the same folder. Rename the newly created file to Item_TwoLinesWithExtraInfo. html. As soon as you save the new filename, refresh the folder. You'll notice that SharePoint automatically created a new file named Item_TwoLinesWithExtraInfo. js. The combination of the HTML and JavaScript file is what makes the magic of display templates come to life. Edit the Item_TwoLinesWithExtraInfo.html file, and change its title to Two Lines with Extra Info.

Getting the new properties

The first code block we should discuss is the `CustomDocumentProperties` block. Let's examine what it holds between its tags:

```
<mso:CustomDocumentProperties>
  <mso:TemplateHidden msdt:dt="string">0</mso:TemplateHidden>
  <mso:ManagedPropertyMapping msdt:dt="string">&#39;Link
    URL&#39;{Link URL}:&#39;Path&#39;,&#39;Line
      1&#39;…</mso:ManagedPropertyMapping>
  <mso:MasterPageDescription msdt:dt="string">This Item Display
    Template will show a small
      thumbnail…</mso:MasterPageDescription>
  <mso:ContentTypeId
    msdt:dt="string">0x0101002039C03B61C64EC4A04F5361F385106603</
mso:ContentTypeId>
  <mso:TargetControlType msdt:dt="string">;#Content Web
    Parts;#</mso:TargetControlType>
  <mso:HtmlDesignAssociated
    msdt:dt="string">1</mso:HtmlDesignAssociated>
  <mso:HtmlDesignConversionSucceeded
    msdt:dt="string">True</mso:HtmlDesignConversionSucceeded>
  <mso:HtmlDesignStatusAndPreview
    msdt:dt="string">https://hippodevssp.sharepoint.com/search/_
catalogs/masterpage/Display%20Templates/Content%20Web%20Parts/Item_
TwoLinesWithExtraInfo.html, Conversion
      successful.</mso:HtmlDesignStatusAndPreview>
</mso:CustomDocumentProperties>
```

The most important properties from this block are:

- **ManagedPropertyMapping**: This property holds all the managed properties that our display template will have access to. The properties are organized in the `key:value` format. For example, if we wish to make use of the Author property, we will declare it as `'Author':'Author'`. The value can be a list of managed properties, so if the first one is null, the mapping will be done using the second one, and so on.

- **ContentTypeId**: This property sets the content type of the display template. The specific value recognizes the file as a display template.

- **TargetControlType**: This property sets the target of the display template. In our example it is set to **Content Web Parts**, which means the search content web part and any other related search content web part. Other possible values are **SearchBox**, **SearchHoverPanel**, **SearchResults**, and so on.

Since we wish to display the author and the last modified date of the document, let's add these two managed properties to the `ManagedPropertyMapping` property. Add the following snippet in the beginning of the property, as follows:

```
<mso:ManagedPropertyMapping

msdt:dt="string">'Author:'Author', 'LastModified':'LastModifiedTime', …
</mso:ManagedPropertyMapping>
```

We mapped the `Author` managed property to the `Author` key, and the `LastModifiedTime` managed property to the `LastModified` key. Next, we will discuss how to actually use the new properties.

Getting the values of the new properties

Using the newly added properties is done using plain old JavaScript.

1. Scroll down a bit until you see the following opening `div` statement:

    ```
    <div id="TwoLines">
    ```

2. The `div` tag begins with what seems to be a comment markup (`<!--`), but if you look closer you should recognize that it is actually JavaScript. By using built-in methods and client object model code, display templates can get any information out of SharePoint, and of the outside world. The `getItemValue` method is in charge of getting content back based on a given managed property. That means if we wish to get the author of a result, and we set the key to the managed property to be `Author`, the following line of code will get it:

    ```
    var author = $getItemValue(ctx, "Author");
    ```

3. The same goes for the last modified date. We used the key `LastModified` for the managed property, and hence the following line of code will be used:

    ```
    var last = $getItemValue(ctx, "LastModified");
    ```

4. Add these two lines just above the closing comment statement markup (`_#-->`).

> Remember that each result is rendered using this display template, so the author and the last variables are unique for that one item that is being rendered.

Displaying the new properties

The last part of the template comes right after the closing comment statement from the previous section. You can see plain old regular HTML at this point, starting with the following line:

```
<div class="cbs-Item" id="_#= containerId =#_"
    data-displaytemplate="Item2Lines">
```

But if you look close enough you might notice something is weird with the `id` property. It has an unusual suffix and prefix. This suffix and prefix are the template placeholders. Whatever value is between these two will get replaced at runtime with the value of its JavaScript variable.

Under the closing `div` tag of `_#= line2Id =#_`, add the following snippet:

```
<div class="cbs-Line2 ms-noWrap"><b>Author: </b>_#= author
    =#_</div>
<div class="cbs-Line2 ms-noWrap"><b>Last Modified: </b>_#= last
    =#_</div>
```

`Author` and `LastModified` are two variables we created in the previous section, and now using the template placeholders we will display them to the users.

Save the new template, and navigate to the site you saved the new template on, which should be the same site to which you added the CSWP earlier as well. Edit the properties of the CSWP and change its display template to our new **Two Lines with Extra Info** custom display template. Click on **OK** and you should get a result similar to the following screenshot:

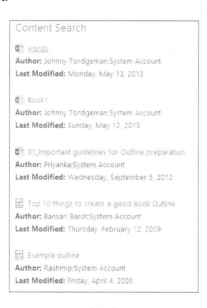

Enriching the Video Games Search Center

If you recall, we created a nice search vertical named **Video Games** in *Chapter 2, Using the Out of the Box Search Components*. The search vertical was scoped to search content in two specific folders we created. One of the fields we could input in our images folder was keyword. By default, SharePoint 2013's images hover panel won't show this field; but as this field is important to us, let's change the display template of that hover panel and add it.

Before we go ahead and create the new result type, head over to your Video Games Center Images folder and add a few keywords to the images of your choice. Once done, wait for the continuous crawl to pick up your changes, or if using an on-premise installation, head over to the search service application and start an incremental crawl, as shown in the previous chapter.

Modifying the default image display template

As we mentioned earlier, the best way to modify a display template is to pick up an out of the box one and modify it. In order to change the image template hover panel, we have to first edit the image display template itself and point it to the new hover panel template we will be creating. To modify the default image display template follow these steps:

1. Launch SharePoint Designer 2013 and open the search center site.

2. Navigate to **Master Page Gallery | Display Templates | Search folder**, and locate the Item_Picture.html file.

3. Once located, copy and paste it in the same folder.

4. Rename the new file to Item_Console_Picture.html. Click on the file and under **Customizations** click on **Edit file**.

5. Change the title of the new template to Console Picture Item.

6. Under the body tag, locate the declaration of the hoverUrl parameter and change it as follows:

```
var hoverUrl =
  "~sitecollection/_catalogs/masterpage/Display
    Templates/Search/Item_Console_Picture_HoverPanel.js";
```

7. Save the file and navigate back to the Search folder.

Now that we have a new image display template, we need to create the new hover panel display template that we had specified for it. To create the new hover panel display template follow these steps:

1. Locate the `Item_Picture_HoverPanel.html` file, copy and paste it in the same folder, and rename it to `Item_Console_Picture_HoverPanel.html`.

2. Edit the file and add the `Keywords` managed property to the `ManagedPropertyMapping` property, just like we did in the previous example. The property should look like the following code:

```
<mso:ManagedPropertyMapping
   msdt:dt="string">'Keywords':'Keywords',&#39;Title&#39;… </
mso:ManagedPropertyMapping>
```

3. Under the div tag in `Item_Picture_HoverPanel.html`, locate the JavaScript section (that begins with `<!--#_`) and before its closing element add the following line of code:

```
var keywords = $getItemValue(ctx, "Keywords");
```

This will get the content of the `Keywords` managed property.

4. To display the value of the `keywords` managed property to the user, add the following lines of code under the span whose ID is:

```
_#= $htmlEncode(id + HP.ids.dimensions) =#_:
<br/>
<b>Keywords: </b> _#= keywords =#_
```

5. Save the file.

We are done with creating the templates, so now it's time to create the result type.

Creating the result type

To create the result type that will match the new display template we created, follow these steps:

1. In your search center, navigate to **Site Settings** and click on **Result Types** under the **Search** section.

2. In the **Manage Result Types** page, click on **New Result Type**. Give the new result type a name such as **Console Picture Type**.

3. For the source select the **Video Games Result** source (reminder: we only wish to have the new display template shown in our search vertical).

4. Click on **Show more conditions** on the left, and choose **Path** as the property. For the operator select **Contains any of** and `<your site url>/VideoGamesImages/` as the value. In our example, the value would be `https://hippodevssp.sharepoint.com/VideoGamesImages/`.

5. For the display type, choose **Console Picture Item**. This is the display template we created in the previous section. Save the result type. Once completed, your settings should look as shown in the following screenshot:

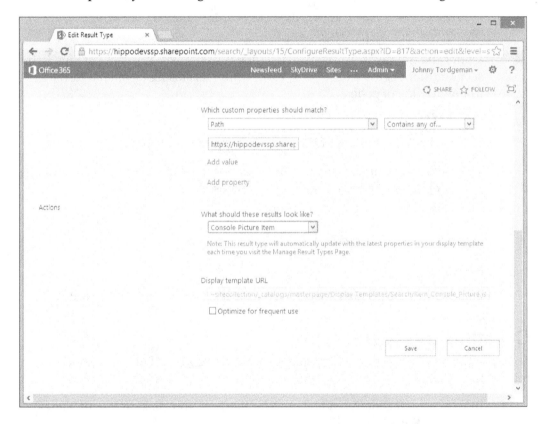

We are now finished with the new result type and display template. Go ahead and perform a search using our **Video Games** search vertical.

Hover over any image result and our new hover panel display template will be shown in all its glory as shown in the following screenshot:

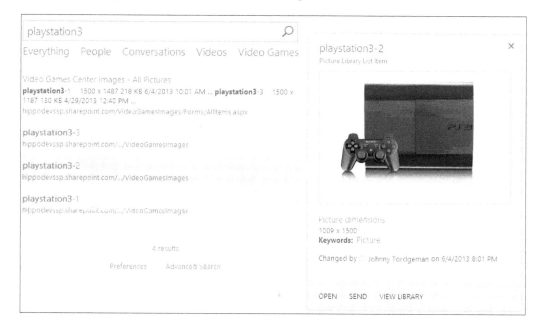

Summary

This chapter was all about prettifying items. We learned about result types and display templates, what the different layers of display templates are, and how to style results in search-related web parts.

We finished the chapter off by creating two new display templates: an item display template based on the **Two lines** out of the box template and a new hover panel display template for the image display template.

Display templates are a powerful feature, and among its popular usages are adding a person's latest status updates whenever someone hovers over their result in the people search, showing the user's latest tweets based on their username, and so on. All of this can be achieved using display templates and a bit of JavaScript client object model.

In the next and final chapter we will discuss the all-important concept of **Business Connectivity Services** (BCS). Using BCS we can get content from external systems and have SharePoint index and search them. So, go get your SQL server ready because we are about to crawl an external database and perform search operations on it.

5
Extending Beyond SharePoint

In this chapter we are going to deal with extending search beyond the scope of SharePoint. So far we've seen search results coming only from within SharePoint, and whether the results were documents, sites, conversations, or images, all came from SharePoint. By leveraging the BCS, we can get SharePoint to index external systems. In this chapter we are going to discuss how to build a .NET assembly BCS that will crawl the external system, and display the results to the user as if they were regular plain old SharePoint results.

In this chapter we will cover the following topics:

- Introduction to BCS in the context of search
- Connecting with the SQL server using .NET assembly

BCS for search

BCS has been in use since SharePoint 2010. If you previously used BCS in SharePoint 2010, you'll feel right at home. As noted before, BCS enables us to connect to external data sources and display the data via web parts, lists, user profile properties, or search.

When discussing BCS we need to understand that BCS is not a technology by itself. It is a grouping term for a set of technologies, which takes care of getting the data from the external system. An external system can be anything from databases (such as SQL server or Oracle) to web services, and even cloud-based solutions.

BCS uses the connectors framework to reach out to external systems. Out of the box, we have four types of connectors we can use straight away: SQL, WCF, .NET, and the newly added OData connector. While the **Business Data Connectivity** (**BDC**) layer is in charge of connecting the external system, it does not know or dictate what data will be returned from the system, or what would its schema look like. All the operations and schema for the returned data are defined by an **external content type** (**ECT**). An ECT specifies the definition of the fields (name and type) that will be returned from the external source. For example, a Product ECT might specify that the data that will be returned from an external system, SQL in this case, as follows:

- **ProductID**: This is an integer representing the unique ID of a product
- **ProductName**: This is a string representing the name of a product
- **ProductPrice**: This is a decimal representing a product's price

In addition to schema definition, an ECT also defines the operations available for the BCS. Just like any modern system, these operations include **Create-Read-Update-Delete** (**CRUD**) operations, and other operations such as file stream reading or getting a list of items.

Now after all this, you may ask yourself what does any of this have to do with search? Good question indeed. BCS is a very broad subject, and can fill out an entire book (and it has), and as we are focused on the subject of search, the rest of the chapter will deal with only search-related aspects of BCS.

 If you wish to go deeper with BCS, check out *Professional Business Connectivity Services in SharePoint 2010*, *Scot Hillier* and *Brad Stevenson*, *Wrox Publishing*. While the book deals with BCS in SharePoint 2010 and not SharePoint 2013, the core concepts are exactly the same.

BCS and search

SharePoint 2013 provides two distinct approaches for processing search queries to return search results: federated and content crawling.

In the federated approach, the results returned by the search query are not crawled (read: stored) by the search server. When we write a search term, the term is forwarded to the external system and then gets processed by it. Once processing is finished, the external system returns the results to SharePoint's search engine, which in turn formats and renders the result. The biggest advantage with federated search is that we don't really need to worry about getting the data to SharePoint, as the external system is in charge of the search logic.

In addition, using federated search we can access systems that don't have the ability to get crawled (or even secured against crawling) but have an internal search engine that is accessible.

Content crawling, on the other hand, returns results from SharePoint's search service application's content index database. This database contains content that was crawled by the search service application, and includes the text content and any metadata the content item may have. Unlike the federated approach, it's our job as developers to get the data into the search service application's index database from the external system. And this is where BCS and search finally meet. Using BCS, we can create a content crawling indexing connector that will bring the external system's data back to SharePoint.

A BCS indexing connector is composed of the following parts:

- **The BDC model file**: This file provides the schema of the data and the connection information to the external system
- **The connector logic**: This is a component that contains the code that connects and crawls the external system

When we develop a BCS indexing connector, it's a good idea to have answers to the following questions:

1. How are we going to connect to the external system? This includes server IP address, database instance name, authentication, and so on.

2. What is the schema of the data we are crawling? How is it organized? What types of fields are we going to crawl? (Think of ECT.)

3. How can we recognize data changes in the repository for the incremental crawl? In order for the crawl to be able to perform incremental search (and by doing that save time and bandwidth) it must have the ability to recognize when content changes in the external system. This is done by either a timestamp-based crawl or change-based log crawl, depending on the external system APIs.

4. Do we need to secure the data we are crawling? In some cases the data we crawl is public and everyone in our organization has access to it. But there are cases where we need to implement a security method, so that users searching through the crawled content will only get results they have access to. This means that our connector must know how to read the permissions of the external system and implement it at crawl time using a Windows **Access Control List** (**ACL**).

The first question is rather easy to answer, as you should be able to get all the information from your IT department, or anyone else that works on maintaining the external system.

When answering the second question we have a few additional parameters to be taken into consideration. As we noted earlier, other than type and name, the ECT also defines operations the BCS will perform. There are six possible operations the BCS can perform, as follows:

- **Finder**: This is a core operation that retrieves a list of items from the external content source that are to be crawled. This method should return minimal information about the items (usually only the ID) and not the entire item content.

- **SpecificFinder**: This is a core operation that retrieves individual items from the external content source based on the list the finder operation generated.

- **ChangedIdEnumerator**: This is an optional operation that returns minimal information (usually ID) about items in the external content source, which were modified after a given time. This is required when implementing a changelog-based incremental crawling.

- **DeletedIdEnumerator**: This is an optional operation that returns minimal information (usually ID) about items in the external content source, which were deleted after a given time. This is required when implementing a changelog-based incremental crawling.

- **BinarySecurityDescriptorAccessor**: This is an optional operation that returns the security descriptor for an item from the external content source. This operation is in charge of handling the security aspects of crawling, and in fact creates the access control lists for each and every item it crawls. This is required if you choose to implement item-level security.

- **StreamAccessor**: This is an optional operation that returns a data stream from a file. When we wish to crawl the content of a file, mostly Office files or PDF, we have to implement a StreamAccessor operation.

Now that we are done with the theory side of BCS in search, let's get active and create a BCS search indexer ourselves!

Building a BCS search connector

Before we begin writing our connector, we need something to connect to. First, extract the downloadable files for this chapter from the Packt Publishing website. You'll notice there is a file called VideoGamesDB.bak. This is a SQL database backup with video games console content that we will crawl to our SharePoint. Restore this database to a SQL server of your choice.

Now that we have content to crawl, let's move on and create the BCS connector.

Setting the operations

As this book is not a book about BCS, we've already created the basics for you. Open the VideoGamesConnector-Starter project from the downloadable content of the book in Visual Studio 2012. The BCS is partially done. What it's missing are a few key factors, as follows:

- Implementation of the ReadList method
- Implementation of the ReadItem method
- Setting the BCS as crawlable

Implementing the ReadList method

Implementing the ReadList method is rather simple. All it does is connect to the database and grab a list of all the items we are going to crawl. Since this is just a preliminary step, we are not going to get all the information about the items, just their IDs. Once the method finishes its run, it returns the list of IDs to the search engine, which in turn will call the ReadItem method for each ID and get the full item content.

Open the DAL class and find the initialization of the _connectionString variable. This variable will hold the connection string for the database hosting the Consoles table. Set the connection string according to your environment.

In this demo we are using a hardcoded value for the connection string. In a real-world application this is not a good idea, as the code moves between environments (developing, testing, production, and so on) and so the connection string changes as well. It is advisable to use SharePoint's Secure Store to store and retrieve this kind of information.

Find the `GetConsolesList` method and implement it as follows:

```
List<VideoGamesEntity> items = new List<VideoGamesEntity>();
SqlConnection sqlConnection = new SqlConnection();
SqlDataReader sqlReader = null;
try
{
sqlConnection = new SqlConnection(_connectionString);
    sqlConnection.Open();
    //Declare Sql Command
    SqlCommand cmd = new SqlCommand();
    cmd.Connection = sqlConnection;

    cmd.CommandText = @"select ID from Consoles";
    sqlReader = cmd.ExecuteReader();

    if (sqlReader.HasRows)
    {
      DataTable dt = new DataTable();
        dt.Load(sqlReader);
        foreach (DataRow row in dt.Rows)
        {
          VideoGamesEntity Entity = new VideoGamesEntity();
            Entity.ID = row["ID"].ToString();
            items.Add(Entity);
        }
    }
    return items;
}
catch (Exception ex)
{
//Write to log
    return items;
}
finally
{
// close reader
    if (sqlReader != null)
    {
      sqlReader.Close();
    }
```

```
      // close connection
      if (sqlConnection != null)
      {
        sqlConnection.Close();
      }
  }
```

The implementation is rather simple. We initiate a new list of the
VideoGamesEntity class, named items. Next we connect to the SQL database
(using the _connectionString variable we initialized earlier) and perform a simple
select query for all the IDs of the Consoles table. Once we have the IDs we add them
to the items list and return the list back to the search engine. Next up we implement
the ReadItem method.

Implementing the ReadItem method

As we noted earlier, the job of the ReadItem method is to bring all the content of a
given item. The method accepts an ID as an argument and uses that ID to bring the
corresponding item.

Locate the GetConsoleItem method and implement it as follows:

```
VideoGamesEntity Entity = new VideoGamesEntity();
SqlConnection EntityConnection = null;
SqlDataReader SqlReader = null;

try
{

//Connection DB
    EntityConnection = new SqlConnection(_connectionString);

//Open Connection (will be closed at the Finally statement)
    EntityConnection.Open();

//Declare Sql Command
    SqlCommand cmd = new SqlCommand();
    cmd.Connection = EntityConnection;
    cmd.CommandText = @"select * from Consoles where ID=@IDParam";

    //Declare Sql Parameters:
```

```
    SqlParameter IDParam = new SqlParameter("@IDParam",
    SqlDbType.Int, 10);
    IDParam.Value = Int32.Parse(id);

//add new parameter to command object
    cmd.Parameters.Add(IDParam);

    SqlReader = cmd.ExecuteReader();
    //Checking if there is any results ( suppose to be only 1 )
    if (SqlReader.HasRows)
    {
      DataTable dt = new DataTable();
        dt.Load(SqlReader);
        DataRow row = dt.Rows[0];

     Entity.ID = id;
        Entity.Title = row["Title"].ToString();
        Entity.Manufacturer = row["Manufacturer"].ToString();
        Entity.HardDisk = row["Hard Disk"].ToString();
        Entity.HighDefinition = bool.Parse(row["High
        Definition"].ToString());
        Entity.Wifi = bool.Parse(row["Wi-fi"].ToString());
        Entity.ImageUrl = row["Image Url"].ToString();
    }
    return Entity;

}
catch (Exception ex)
{
//Write to log
    return Entity;
}
finally
{
// close reader
    if (SqlReader != null)
    {
      SqlReader.Close();
    }

    // close connection
    if (EntityConnection != null)
    {
      EntityConnection.Close();
    }
}
```

No rocket science here. For each item from the `ReadList` method, the `ReadItem` method gets called. The method connects to the SQL server and performs a select query filtered by the given ID. Once results come back from SQL, we create a `VideoGamesEntity` entity and set its properties. Finally we return the data filled entity to the search engine for crawling. The search engine receives the new entity and stores the new entity in the search index database. We now implemented the two basic operations needed for BCS to operate. The next step is to set the connector to be crawlable, or in other words, search enabled.

Making the BCS model crawlable

The BCS model has several properties that we can set which are related to search. These properties include the following:

- **ShowInSearchUI**: This is a model-level property that specifies that this model should be displayed in the search user interface. The value of this property is ignored; what's important is the inclusion of the property itself in the model. This property is required when building a searchable BCS model.

- **InputUriProcessor / OutputUriProcessor**: These are LobSystem level properties, which enable custom processing of the input and output URLs before passing it to the search system or connector.

- **RootFinder**: This is a method-level property which specifies the default Finder method that the connector should use to enumerate the items for crawling. This property is required for a searchable BCS model.

- **DirectoryLink / AttachmentAccessor**: These are two method-level properties, which are used for creating association between entities. It is recommended that you read the post on the blog regarding related entities at `http://blog.johnnyt.me/2013/03/crawling-with-fast-and-sharepoint-2013/`.

- **AuthorField**: This is a method-level property that specifies the author name to display in the search results. This is usually set in the `SpecificFinder` method to point to the field from the external content source that should be used for displaying the author.

- **DisplayUriField**: This is a method-level property that specifies the URL to show in the search results for a given item. This property overrides the default profile page URL that the BCS service sets.

- **DescriptionField**: This is a method-level property that specifies the description to display for the result.

There are many more properties we can set for our searchable BCS and you can find more information about them at the MSDN documentation page located at `http://msdn.microsoft.com/en-us/library/gg294165.aspx`.

The first property we will set is the `ShowInSearchUI` property. Double-click on the `VideoGamesModel.bdcm` file and switch the tab to **BDC Explorer**. Navigate to the **VideoGamesModel LOBSystemInstance** and click on the three dots (...) next to **Custom Properties** as shown in the following screenshot:

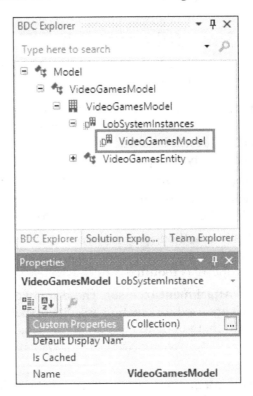

Add a new property named `ShowInSearchUI`, and set the type to `System.String` and the value to `x`.

Next, we will set up the `RootFinder` property. In the BDC explorer pane, navigate to the `ReadList` method. On the **BDC Method Details** pane (usually in the bottom area) locate the `ReadList` instance and click on the three dots (**...**) next to **Custom properties**, as shown in the following screenshot:

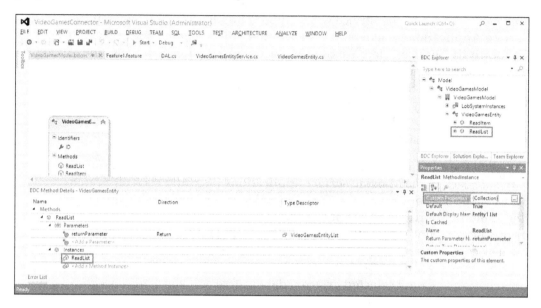

Add a new property named `RootFinder` with a type of `System.String` and a value of x.

Build and deploy the solution. If everything goes smoothly, continue to the next section where we set the permissions and a content source of the newly added searchable BCS.

Creating a search content source

Now that we have a BCS connector ready for crawling, it's time to create a content source that will use it. Head over to your server's SharePoint 2013 Central Administration and click on **Manage service applications**. From the list of service applications, click on the service whose type is **Business Data Connectivity Service Application** (in a default installation it will be named **Business Data Connectivity Service**). Here we can see a list of installed BCS models, and among these we should find our searchable BCS model **VideoGamesEntity**. Whenever we deploy a BCS model we have to set its permissions. Check the checkbox next to the **VideoGamesEntity** model and click on **Set Object Permissions** on the ribbon. Add the farm administrator account and give it all the available permissions. Add the Everyone account and give it permissions to execute.

Now that the administrative part is behind us, let's create the content source. Navigate back to the **Manage service applications** page and click on **Search Service Application**. Under the **Crawling** category on the left-side menu, you'll find **Content Sources**. Click on it to navigate to the content sources management page. Click on **New Content Source**. The **Add Content Source** page appears. Give the new content source the title `Video Games Content Source`. The type of our new content source is **Line of Business Data**, as we are using a BCS source. Change the radio button to **Crawl selected external data source** and check the checkbox next to **VideoGamesModel**, which is our BCS model as shown in the following screenshot:

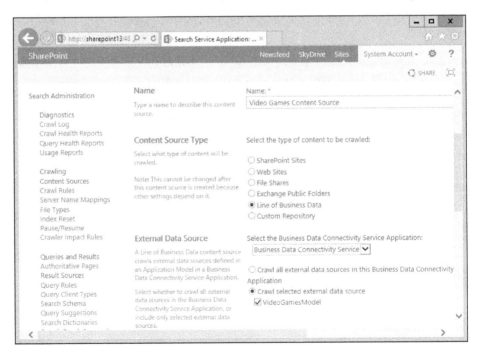

Scroll all the way to the bottom of the page and click on **OK**. Our new content source is ready! To perform a crawl, click on the little arrow to the right of the content source name and click on **Start Full Crawl**. The content source will start crawling. Once the status changes to **Idle**, check the **Crawl Log** page. If your content source had seven successes, everything went great. Try to perform a search for xbox. You'll get a result similar to the following screenshot:

This weird looking result you are seeing is a result from an external content source. It is easily identified by the unusual looking URL it has.

When we perform a custom crawl we automatically create crawled properties. Crawled properties represent the BCS model entity's properties. For our entity, we have automatically created a number of crawled properties such as the **ImageUrl**, **Title**, and so on. Crawled properties for a BCS model have an easy-to-remember syntax: `<BCS model name>.<Entity name>`, that is `videogamesmodel.Title`.

In order to display the crawled properties, we have to map the crawled properties to managed properties. That is done through the **Search Schema** page. Head back to the **Search Service Application** page, click on **Search Schema**, and then on **New Managed Property**. We will map the **ImageUrl** crawled property to a new managed property named `ConsoleImageUrl`, so type `ConsoleImageUrl` in the **Property Name** textbox. The type of the crawled property is text (string in the entity model class). The following main characteristics section defines how this property is going to be treated:

- Searchable means that the property is included in the full text index. This means that if the managed property value contains the word `Console`, searching for `Console` will return the result.

- Queryable is very similar to searchable, but does not offer a full text index. That means that if the property value is `Console`, only searching for `propertyname:Console` will return the result.

- Retrievable means that the managed property will be returned as part of the search result. If we are going to use result types and display templates (which we should always consider) we have to mark the property as retrievable.

- Refineable means that we can use this managed property in the refinement panel and refine the results based on this property.

- Sortable means that we can sort the results based on this property.

Since we are not planning on performing a search based on the URL of an item, the only characteristics we wish to add to the managed property is Retrievable.

The most important part of mapping a managed property is, well, mapping it. Under the **Mappings to crawled properties** section, click on the **Add a Mapping** button to bring up the mapping popup. Filter the categories to **Business Data** to see all the available crawled properties as can be seen in the following screenshot:

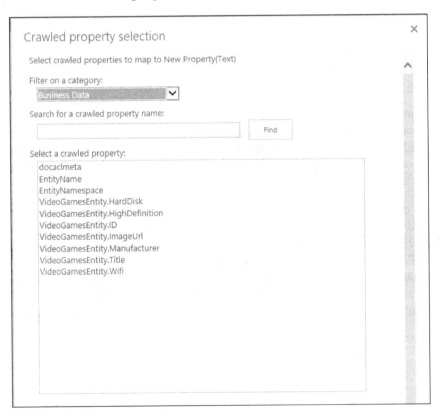

The property we are after is `VideoGamesEntity.ImageUrl`, so select it and click on **OK**. Click on **OK** again to save the new managed property.

In order to use the new managed property, perform another full crawl on the related content source.

Once the crawl is finished, create a new result type and display template to retrieve the new managed property and proudly display it to the users.

Summary

This was a pretty intensive chapter, but we hope you managed to soak in most, if not all, of what it aimed to provide. Creating a BCS connector might seem like a daunting task at first, but the more connectors you create, and the more you play around with its different methods and variables, the more you will learn to love it. Using BCS connectors we get the ultimate power of crawling external systems, a task which used to be next to impossible in the past.

This chapter also brings our little book to an end. We hope you enjoyed working with search, and we are sure that you will take everything you learned into an exciting real-world project that combines with, or is completely based on, search.

Index

W

web front end 12
Web service callout 12

X

XRANK 38
XRANK keyword 25
XSLT 59

Thank you for buying
Learning Search-driven Application Development with SharePoint 2013

About Packt Publishing

Packt, pronounced 'packed', published its first book "Mastering phpMyAdmin for Effective MySQL Management" in April 2004 and subsequently continued to specialize in publishing highly focused books on specific technologies and solutions.

Our books and publications share the experiences of your fellow IT professionals in adapting and customizing today's systems, applications, and frameworks. Our solution based books give you the knowledge and power to customize the software and technologies you're using to get the job done. Packt books are more specific and less general than the IT books you have seen in the past. Our unique business model allows us to bring you more focused information, giving you more of what you need to know, and less of what you don't.

Packt is a modern, yet unique publishing company, which focuses on producing quality, cutting-edge books for communities of developers, administrators, and newbies alike. For more information, please visit our website: www.packtpub.com.

About Packt Enterprise

In 2010, Packt launched two new brands, Packt Enterprise and Packt Open Source, in order to continue its focus on specialization. This book is part of the Packt Enterprise brand, home to books published on enterprise software – software created by major vendors, including (but not limited to) IBM, Microsoft and Oracle, often for use in other corporations. Its titles will offer information relevant to a range of users of this software, including administrators, developers, architects, and end users.

Writing for Packt

We welcome all inquiries from people who are interested in authoring. Book proposals should be sent to author@packtpub.com. If your book idea is still at an early stage and you would like to discuss it first before writing a formal book proposal, contact us; one of our commissioning editors will get in touch with you.

We're not just looking for published authors; if you have strong technical skills but no writing experience, our experienced editors can help you develop a writing career, or simply get some additional reward for your expertise.

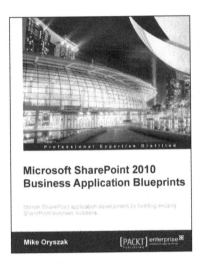

Microsoft SharePoint 2010 Business Application Blueprints

ISBN: 978-1-84968-360-9   Paperback: 282 pages

Master SharePoint application development by building exciting SharePoint business solutions

1. Instant SharePoint – Build nine exciting SharePoint business solutions

2. Expand your knowledge of the SharePoint platform so that you can tailor the sample solutions to your requirements

3. Learn how the different development techniques can be used in various situations to support both client side and server side development to solve different problems in different environments.

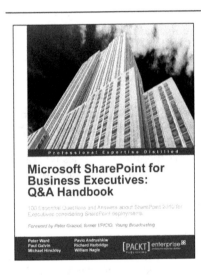

Microsoft SharePoint for Business Executives: Q&A Handbook

ISBN: 978-1-84968-610-5   Paperback: 236 pages

100 Essential Questions and Answers about SharePoint 2010 for Executives considering SharePoint deployments

1. Forget lengthy technical SharePoint guides more suited for hands-on technical staff; get equipped with the knowledge of SharePoint's business potential before deployment

2. Get to grips with SharePoint governance, the Cloud, staffing, development and much more from a business perspective in this book and e-book

Please check **www.PacktPub.com** for information on our titles

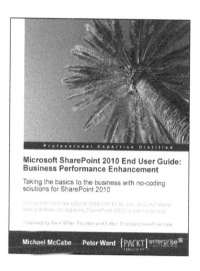

Microsoft SharePoint 2010 End User Guide: Business Performance Enhancement

ISBN: 978-1-84968-066-0   Paperback: 424 pages

A from-the-trenches tutorial filled with hints, tips, and real world best practices for applying SharePoint 2010 to your business

1. Designed to offer applicable, no-coding solutions to dramatically enhance the performance of your business

2. Excel at SharePoint intranet functionality to have the most impact on you and your team

3. Drastically enhance your End user SharePoint functionality experience

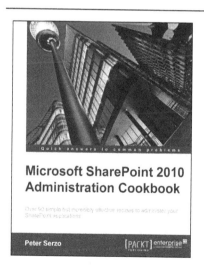

Microsoft SharePoint 2010 Administration Cookbook

ISBN: 978-1-84968-108-7   Paperback: 288 pages

Over 90 simple but incredibly effective recipes to administer your SharePoint applications

1. Solutions to the most common problems encountered while administering SharePoint in book and eBook formats

2. Upgrade, configure, secure, and back up your SharePoint applications with ease

3. Packed with many recipes for improving collaboration and content management with SharePoint

Please check **www.PacktPub.com** for information on our titles